ADVENTURE TALES
OF MONTANA'S
LAST FRONTIER

Also by Gary A. Wilson

*Tiger of the Wild Bunch: The Life and Death of
Harvey "Kid Curry" Logan*

Long George Francis: Gentleman Outlaw of Montana

Honky-Tonk Town: Havre, Montana's Lawless Era

Outlaw Tales of Montana

ADVENTURE TALES OF MONTANA'S LAST FRONTIER

BY GARY A. WILSON

RIVERBEND
PUBLISHING

Dedicated
to the late
Arlie J. Lane,
one of Havre's finest.

James 1:17

Adventure Tales of Montana's Last Frontier
text © 2013 Gary A. Wilson
Published by Riverbend Publishing, Helena, Montana

ISBN 13: 978-1-60639-071-9
Printed in the United States of America.

3 4 5 6 7 8 9 VP 20 19 18 17

Unless otherwise credited, all photographs were supplied by the author.

Cover design by Sarah Cauble, sarahegrant.com
Text design by Barbara Fifer

Contents

Acknowledgments

I cannot ever say enough about the research and moral support I have received over the years from the Havre-Hill County Library's highly professional staff. Bonnie Williamson, the now-retired head librarian, has made contributions beyond the library's scope with her knowledge of the area; also always helpful are Antoinette "Toni" Hagener and Jim Spangelo, whose knowledge of the area goes beyond mine.

And too, Shari Robinson, whose typing and editing skills were necessary to put these (and Harvey "Kid Curry" Logan) stories on paper.

Also, my appreciation to Nancy Lee Jennings of the Johnson County Library in Buffalo, Wyoming, who helped me extensively in researching the Ranger family, and gave me a tour of the area.

And to those who helped me with the very last minute picture gathering and processing: Val Hickman of Vande Bogart Library Montana State University–Northern, and Heather Parker of Helmbrecht Studio.

While I have all these (and more) people to thank, the ultimate responsibility for the facts and interpretations of history developed in this book rests entirely with me.

I hope to continue to play some small part in the preservation of western history in northern Montana.

Gary A. Wilson
Bullhook Sidings (Havre)
July 2013

Foreword

The drive from Bainville to Browning is long and lonely. At night the Canadian border security lights flicker in the distance. Lights of occasional small towns appear on the dark horizon, as the stars pass in silent cascade across the long sky. The winding Milk River reflects with burnished glow the sky's dust. Across the flat plan, a line of dark trees marks the water course of the Missouri. Sudden mountains disturb the horizon with bizarre, almost mystical shapes—the Little Rockies, Bear's Paw, the Sweet Grass Hills. Small towns—Culbertson, Saco, Dodson, Rudyard—provide welcome coffee breaks in the long night, while larger towns—Glasgow, Havre, Shelby, Cut Bank—bring traffic lights, police cars, four-lane streets. The Indian towns of Browning, Frazer, Poplar, Fort Belknap, are reminders of another culture in this land of wheat, cattle, oil, the railroad. Separated from "mainstream" Montana by the Missouri River, the Hi-Line is a country unto itself.

Harrison Lane
Professor, Northern Montana College, Havre
Montana Magazine, *May-June, 1985*

Introduction

The myriads of ducks, geese and other waterfowl scattered, and sage hens took to the sagebrush flats as the heavy-laden wagons with their sweat-soaked horses straining at their traces approached the river bottoms. The wildlife of this area would have to find another portion of the Milk River for a watering hole.

The wagons contained the supplies and materials necessary to set up camp and build a log trading post to be called Fort Belknap. Enough logs had to be obtained from the nearby Bear's Paw Mountains for a surrounding stockade, trading store building, school, doctor's quarters, laundry room, mess hall, barracks, stable, blacksmith shop—and of course, the Indian agent's quarters.

There would be no worries from the local Indian population, because the Gros Ventres (White Clay People), upper Canadian Assiniboine (Nakota), and River Crow (Absaroka) were on this land by treaty. They welcomed the nearby fort to their west, because it would lessen the Lakota Sioux attacks when treaty goods arrived. Besides, this large military fort—called Assinniboine, with a spelling unique to the army, under General Order #9, December 30, 1878—soon would dominate the landscape.

The 1873 post was later managed for the Durfee and Peck Company by thirty-year-old Irishman Thomas O'Hanlon, who had operated the trading post at Fort Peck, eastward on the Missouri River. Also at the trading post was resident Indian agent Major W.L. Lincoln, whose wife was the first white woman in the area. O'Hanlon, and his assistant, Louis Bogy, claimed squatter's rights to a hill two miles north of the post, for a town where the railroad station of Dawes then stood. The spot became the town of Chinook and the money from lot sales went into a school district fund. O'Hanlon established a large general store, and eventually he went into the history books as the "Father of Chinook."

The Milk River Country would never be the same, as white settlers poured into Montana's last frontier, building farms, ranches and towns like Chinook, where North American Indians and buffalo once freely roamed.

The preamble to an old black-and-white television detective series set in New York City began with "There are over a million stories in the Naked City." The Milk River Country of north-central Montana never accrued that many stories, but does hold numerous fascinating stories of the few thousands who entered the area after 1888. Some of these stories have never been put on paper, even though the families always meant to. Some families had personal histories in loose sheets or notebooks, others held scattered papers that eventually made it to the "round file." How sad.

The Milk River, lifeline of the region, begins in the peaks of Glacier National Park. Two forks of the river flow northeastward into the Canadian province of Alberta, where they merge. Then the Milk flows about 170 miles eastward, where the waterway re-enters Montana near the Alberta-Saskatchewan border north of Rudyard, Montana. The Milk then meanders about 50 miles to the ancient riverbed of the Missouri River, west of the town of Havre. From there, the stream continues east about 300 miles to Nashua, where Porcupine Creek joins it and it turns south for 70 miles, traveling near the western boundary the Fort Peck Indian Reservation until it joins the Missouri River—a total journey of nearly 700 miles.

The only fame that the river can claim is it was named by the Lewis and Clark Expedition because its mouth on the Missouri looked like "a cup of tea with a spoonful of milk." The Milk was selected as one of the first projects of the Newlands Reclamation

Act of 1902. This led to formal irrigation districts along its length from Lohman-Chinook to Nashua. Later came dams, reservoirs and additional water from the St. Mary's River of Canada.

Milk River Country is also dubbed the "High Line" or "Hi-Line." The surveyors of the Great Northern Railway named it because of the rails' ascent from Havre to the Marias Pass summit of the Rocky Mountains' Continental Divide in Glacier National Park. Eventually that name extended as far east as Williston, North Dakota.

Some of this prairie country opened to settlement in 1887, and more the following year when Fort Belknap and Fort Peck Indian reservations were reduced to their current dimensions. At one time the whole north country had belonged to the Blackfoot nation; the Gros Ventres and upper (Canadian) Assiniboine now occupy some of this land. The River Crow went south to join the Mountain Crow.

Once the rich grasslands opened, Texas longhorns and Oregon shorthorns poured into the country by cattle drive and railroad. The cattle spread across the area from Clear Creek near Yantic (now Lohman) to the North Dakota and Canada borders. Milk River Country's mountains, buttes and foothills, and small, shallow valleys and coulees offered protection from harsh winter storms and their accompanying arctic winds.

Locals considered this country one of the best cattle-raising regions in the United States, ranking in grazing quality with the Sand Hills of Nebraska. Besides the grazing, Milk River Country is known for its high-grade wheat, barley and other grains.

The early Great Northern Railway stations became the towns and cattle-shipping centers of the north country. East of the railroad center of Havre were other important railroad freight and passenger points at Yantic (Lohman), Harlem, Zurich, Dodson and Wagner, as well as Malta and Glasgow in Valley County.

The Havre area was originally part of the large Fort Assinniboine Military Reservation from the Milk River south to the Bear's Paw Mountains. The reservation's only inhabitants were supposed to be soldiers, civilian workers and teamsters, but the large land area was too tempting. People began to bring their livestock in.

These pioneers drawn to the Milk River's frontier were little different from the people who had settled other agricultural sections of the West. They all had their hopes and dreams of a better life, knowing too that they would have to face adversity. Along with them also came the dregs of society, who would only add to their burden.

In *Trial and Triumph: 101 Years In North Central Montana* (published by North Central Chinook Cow Belles, 1968), author Janet Allison speaks of this country originally thought fit only for "steers and bachelors," but then you read of the men and women who invested their lives in the region to make it better than that— and they succeeded.

Allison dedicates the book in part, "To them, the hardy, hopeful ones who lived and live here." I can do no better. I hope the current book holds stories with her richness.

Army Chaplain's Wife

Eliza Shaw Dodd, 1881-1883

OLD GLORY, FLAPPING in the cool fall breeze, had hung at half-mast since the command at Fort Assinniboine received word of President James A. Garfield's death on September 19, 1881. Garfield had been struck down by an assassin's bullet in Washington, D.C., while the Ohio-born president awaited a train to his East Coast home in Elferon, New Jersey, but had lingered for two and a half miserable months.

On a day of national mourning, Chaplain Stephen Dodd presented a eulogy at the new chapel/school building. Wife Eliza wrote that her husband centered his talk around Jeremiah 48:17 of the Old Testament, using the analogy of the ancient kingdom of Jordan's destruction. It can be translated, "Bemoan him, all you who are around him, all who know his name; see how the mighty scepter is broken, the glorious staff."

Brand-new Fort Assinniboine chapel, complete with lightning rod. PHOTOGRAPH BY FRITZ STUDIO, HAVRE, COURTESY OF MONTANA HISTORICAL SOCIETY PHOTOGRAPH ARCHIVES, HELENA, MT

She started the first page of her new diary with, "This is the commencement of a new year for me." Thus she started in 1881 with the September death of the president, her fifty-third birthday and the first snowfall—a month earlier than usual. This probably added to the somber tone of the day in spite of the cards and presents, causing her to have no appetite for food, cake or candy.

The Dodd family, with grown son Amzi, had arrived at the fort in June of 1879, and would not have joined the trek west with the 18th Infantry from Atlanta, Georgia, since a chaplain was assigned to a station, not a unit. Besides, Dodd had only recently enlisted as an army chaplain, leaving behind his Presbyterian Church in Salt Lake City. Hence their vehicle for a more leisurely trip was a narrow gauge train of the Utah-Northern Railroad to Helena, Montana, then a wagon ride north to the tent city where Fort Assinniboine was being built on Beaver Creek. The camp was located some forty miles south of the "British Possessions line," between where Beaver Creek flowed into the Milk River and the Bear's Paw Mountains in north central Montana Territory.

Like many in the military, the Dodd family was a long way from home and civilization. Stephen's family hailed from the Bloomfield, New Jersey, area, while Eliza's family called Marietta, Ohio, home. The Dodds belonged to the Presbyterian Church of the U.S.A., the denomination's non-secessionist branch, and they were involved with the Princeton Theological Seminary.

Stephen began his studies there at the age of twenty-two, as an "officer and tutor," received his divinity degree in 1851, and was ordained in 1852. The following year he married Eliza in Cleveland, Ohio, and served New England churches before moving on to Salt Lake City, and Boise, Idaho.

Eliza's history is less clear. She was born in Marietta in September of 1830. She apparently attended and then taught at the Cooper Female Academy of Dayton, Ohio. Montana women's history researcher Loy Chvilicek hypothesizes that since there was a U.S. Central Branch Soldier's Home in Dayton, perhaps Stephen spent some time there as a chaplain's intern, and met Eliza.

Their son, Amzi, named after an uncle, was born in Boise in August 1855. They returned to the northeast, where Dodd served as a chaplain with the Massachusetts 25th Volunteer Infantry during the latter stages of the Civil War. They moved farther south to a church at Middleboro, after Stephen was mustered out of the army in 1866. His last ministry before joining the US Army was at Salt Lake City, hardly a Presbyterian bastion. Possibly he joined the army for better pay and more-permanent assignments. At the time the nation was suffering from the major financial depression misnamed the Panic of 1873, making military service an attractive career choice.

The family arrived at the Beaver Creek campsite, where the 18th Infantry, 2nd Cavalry, Quartermaster and Engineer Corps from St. Paul, and civilian workers, were being organized into a building force. Eliza's diary began two and one-quarter years later when the fort included sixty-three of the hundred-some buildings eventually completed. At that time Eliza was fifty-one, Stephen five years older, and Amzi twenty-seven years old. Also originally occupying their new quarters were two women, one a cook, the other a servant. These women left by 1881, replaced by a husband-wife team.

The Dodds would have occupied one of the company duplex quarters on Officer's Row by the fall of 1879. The downstairs consisted of a kitchen with a pantry and china closet, with stairs to the cellar, a dining room and parlor (living room) with a fireplace. Upstairs in the attic were two bedrooms, a bathroom and the servant's quarters to the rear. The quarters soon had piped-in water with radiator heat and, much later, a sewer system for toilets and latrines. Soldiers daily delivered ice, water and wood for the stove and fireplace.

The quarters were Eliza's bailiwick while Stephen presided over the chapel/school. He kept busy as the school superintendent, with morning classes for enlisted men, civilian employees and others, and separate classes for officers' and trading post managers' children. In the afternoons, other enlisted men took over, with some hundred soldiers learning reading, writing, arithmetic, civics and science (by Dodd) under four instructors. Of course Dodd planned the curriculum, and trained and supervised the instructors. The Fort Benton newspaper vaguely described him as gray-haired and bearded.

The reading and writing were particularly important since each company and the headquarters required a literate clerk. And, the military attracted many Europeans and Britons who needed instruction in American English. The army provided little in school supplies, making instruction quite a challenge. Since Eliza paid for the art supplies her students used, Stephen probably chipped in for other school supplies, and the fort library offered magazines and newspapers.

In addition there were the Sunday services and Bible classes, which Eliza taught for all the children. For Stephen there were other duties including counseling, marriages, funerals, baptisms and officially recording the rites. Unlike other officers and wives, Stephen and Eliza met with people from both sides of the tracks, since they ministered to all, including laundresses (mostly enlisted men's wives) and resident Indian families.

Son Amzi worked for the post trading company of C.A. Broadwater and R.L. McCulloh as a bookkeeper/purchasing clerk. His job consisted of keeping track of the store's received goods and contracting for fort supplies, which made him one busy man.

The partners' firm consisted of a large retail store with warehouses attached on two sides, and an officers club in the rear. Nearby was a small building used for trading furs and hides with the Indian populace. Within the vast complex were a saloon, hotel, restaurant, photography shop, telegraph office, barbershop, stagecoach office, and post office. The store contained a great variety of merchandise from all over the East and abroad, except for materials the women needed to make clothing. These had to be mail ordered from the "states." A stagecoach brought the mail from Fort Benton three times a week, weather permitting, and the firm's merchandise came from Fort Benton's Missouri River docks by bull train. They also operated the wood camp in the mountains with Indian laborers, and provided the beef from their own herd and slaughterhouse.

Amzi participated in trying to develop a civilian town north on Big Sandy Creek. At first the development, known as "Assinaboine City," was to be erected close to the Milk River, where a Power Brothers trading post was once located, but that site proved too remote. The post was moved south and renamed "Cypress," because it was the crossing for the freight wagons on their way to Fort Walsh, the Northwest Mounted Police post and adjacent trading store in Saskatchewan's Cypress Hills. The second "city" just outside the military reserve boundary contained saloons, brothels and a hardware store owned by Frank Cowan. He relocated to Bremer at the Box Elder stage station. Whether or not this town-building was an official duty of Amzi's is not known.

While all the commercial and military operations were carried on by men, the wives of the officers and post traders established a traditional upper-class social life, described as "an aristocracy by selection and the halo of tradition." This circle had its own stylized code of conduct, above and beyond those of others who frequented the fort or lived in the area. The army categorized all the women as camp followers—the same designation as for prostitutes—and their presence received no official recognition.

But the women's group provided more than superficial status, being part of a tight-knit source of emotional strength as families contended with the harsh and dangerous elements of the wilds, including a bleak climate and isolation from friends, family and civilization. There was a daily fear of injury from accidents, and the constant dangers of combat injuries or lost or frostbitten soldiers. And too, the unseen dangers of bacterial, fungal, viral and parasitic diseases assaulted the settlement constantly. European medical advances were only beginning to filter through the few legitimate eastern medical schools.

These ladies presumably cemented their relationships early because of the harsh living conditions in the prairie tent city.

The combined heat, drought, record mosquito infestation, dust storms and putrid water made them reliant on each other. Happily, though, Major J.C. Lee of the Quartermaster Corps supported their social affairs by providing a spacious tent with a wooden floor covered with a polished canvas cover. In addition, the post trading company made sure they received all the food delicacies that could be provided in a can. Once the fort was completed, they lived in luxury compared to many other forts in the West.

Of all the women's preserved writings about the fort, however, only Eliza's diary gives us a daily view into their lives at Fort Assinniboine.

The saddest part of that first diary section, in late September 1881, was about the first snowfall and how it meant the nearing end of flower beds, gardens, picnics, fishing trips, and shopping in Fort Benton. Rare trips to the wealthy territorial capital city of Helena were especially coveted. Eliza particularly enjoyed evening walks with Stephen up and down the wooden boardwalk, which went from the general store north to the chapel/school, and beyond to end at the hospital. A boardwalk also crossed the parade grounds to the headquarters and went on to the commissary store. Sometimes fort residents took a really ambitious walk to the hills outside the fort and along Beaver Creek, where wildflowers grew.

The commissary provided their food staples, but food luxuries came from the general store. Its vast shelves contained groceries, utensils, cleaning supplies, hardware, clothing and shoes, tobacco, liquor, meats and fish, and fruits and vegetables when in season. The post trader's store and post office were frequent visiting places for the women.

Eliza's diary listed her shopping trips and pleasure walks, and noted the need to buy additional items by mail from eastern firms. A once- or twice-daily weather record was a must, along with details about daily visitors and visits, whether formal or informal. These visits usually meant a gift exchange of pies, cakes, bread or candy. Sometimes they included crocheting, exchanging books, or mending and sewing clothing. The Dodds' evenings included the walks when weather permitted, chess games, and social or military events, such as the summer dress parades and close order drills. The other ladies' lives more closely followed the post's daily bugle calls, which began at dawn and continued through evening, to the retreat at sunset, followed by tattoo and taps at about 9:00 P.M. Eliza sometimes stayed up until the wee hours reading books, and always commented of her weakness in the following day's diary entry. Books, magazines and newspapers were a large part of their lives—and, of course, letters from home, which were read over and over.

Other details she recorded were buying milk-product tickets from nearby Herron's Farm, and what she ate for meals—many times having a brunch if Stephen or Amzi did not come home for midday "dinner." She always gave a general count and breakdown of who attended church and Bible class, and what Stephen preached about. She wrote of those participating in her art classes, personal drawing/painting time, and the supplies she regularly sent for.

Rarely did she express any negatives, but the new husband and wife servants received an almost full-page tirade because of "… their uppity behavior" and his drinking and wife abuse. But servants were scarce, and much tolerance was necessary. A visiting McCulloh niece received criticism (or pity) because her hair was hanging long and straight down, lessening her beauty. Also, one officer's wife insisted on singing loud and off-key during church services, making for a less joyous sound to the Lord. Yet in the main, Eliza expressed much caring and concern for her companions.

Officers and their families came and went to new assignments, temporary duty elsewhere, or to military schools. Hence, the women's circle had to be readjusted frequently. Some were only Eliza's acquaintances but others being close friends. One entry told of the unhappiness of Lieutenant Gustavus Doane's wife, Mary, with her husband's being called out on patrol all the time because the other cavalry first lieutenant had summer duty at Camp Coal

Banks. Doane is best known for his involvement in early exploration of future Yellowstone National Park; he also commanded the first Howgate polar expedition to Greenland in 1880. Doane died in 1892, while Mary lived until 1952.

The women's special activities weren't perfected until the Officers Amusement Hall was built in 1886 by troop labor. Until then their quarters, enlisted men's hall/gym and even the hospital had been used. As one officer's wife at Fort Shaw described social life there, "… almost everyday there is a dinner or card party… given…" Eliza described them as "…quite elegant, formal affairs, beautifully serene with dainty chosen and handsome selves." She added that the officers were not comfortable in their full dress uniforms. She concluded that everyone was happy in the fall when the summer campaign concluded and everyone settled down for winter and the wining and dining began.

But the winters weren't all fun and games. Occasionally a winter patrol or full complement of troops went out, usually to eastward trouble spots along Frenchman's Creek and the Little Rocky Mountains. By 1881, the mainly western Teton-Lakota native peoples across the border had surrendered and were living on reservations in the Dakota Territory, leaving the "British Indians" and Métis (mixed blood French-Indian people) to deal with. Eliza wrote that just after the troops left in October, the wooden floor under the hospital's heated bathtub caught fire; chimney fires were also common.

The soldiers rarely came back with bullet wounds, although frozen limbs were quite common, resulting at times in failed surgeries and even death.

On October 10, Eliza wrote of taking medicine for the pain that kept her awake at night, perhaps a patent medicine that equaled whiskey in alcohol content. Or it could have been opiate, quinine or mercury pills. For serious health problems, harsh laxatives and emetics were given by older physicians, although there were a few enlightened European-trained medicos.

Son Amzi was briefly mentioned at times, but he put in long

hours for the post trading operation, although Eliza mentions an occasional late night he spent talking (drinking) and smoking cigars with McCulloh. The harsh winters required him to travel and come up with an extra amount of hay for the post's livestock. He apparently spent his leisure time with the bachelor officers, but when he came home, he brought treats—especially fresh fruit, a preventive for scurvy.

For several weeks there were entries about Eliza's asking Stephen to have a carpenter repair a shelf. Eventually he remembered to take it, and she put it up herself, just before their wedding anniversary. Actually Eliza had forgotten that day until two gold coins—from son and husband—dropped out of her dinner napkin. She spent the rest of evening playing chess with a Mrs. M.B. Miller, wife of First Lieutenant W.A. Miller. The Millers had spent the past summer at the Coal Banks Steamboat Landing camp.

In early December 1881, there was excitement on Officers Row when several homes were burglarized; criminals in the army ranks weren't uncommon. A Mrs. Wheeler calmed things down by giving a talk on the Indian peoples she had interviewed at the Coal Banks camp, including White Eagle.

November 4 was a typically busy day, its entry starting with a notation of what a beautiful day it was. First on the agenda was baking a cake and gingerbread. One wife was ill, staying in bed until noon, but Eliza stayed busy trying to make an easel with her painting partner, Mrs. Bates. Unfortunately their carpentry skills weren't up to it, and Stephen would have another project to take to a post carpenter. She went to the post office to mail a letter, and returned with lots of newspapers, but not letters. The rest of the day was taken up with callers. She stayed up after midnight reading the latest acquired book, *Fugitives*.

A Sunday dinner was ruined by her servants' "acting like ninnies"—no specifics given. The next day was shopping at both the commissary and post trader's store.

With Christmas approaching, the Dodds decided to spruce

up their parlor with a new carpet, but neither of them had the strength to stretch it out and nail it down. Again, they would need the services of a post carpenter.

In other entries, she brought prairie chickens from the "bandman," a member of the post military band. After she recorded making squash and plum pies she wrote sadly "Stewart to lose feet." According to the 1880 census, Francis Stewart was the First Sergeant of the 2nd Cavalry; thirty-nine years old, single and from Scotland. She noted a few days later that Stewart didn't survive the surgery and was buried with full military honors—and life went on.

The Dodds' best friends seemed to be the "Norwoods," captain and wife; only the census calls them "Noriwind." He was listed as forty-five and she twenty-nine, a fellow Ohioan. Norwood joined Dodd on hunting trips or rides in the country. A big event occurred when Mrs. Norwood received a piano, and calling cards went out. Usually such furniture was reserved for the commander, since lesser officers had to pay their own freight.

The third closely followed event, besides the piano and Stewart's burial, Eliza mentioned a sickness among the women, but gave no details. Always she recorded food preparation, one of her lengthiest entries covering seeding raisins. New clothing was necessary for Christmas, requiring materials to be ordered, some from Boston.

At times, Stephen's ministry outreach was mentioned. Eliza joined him on most visits, such as to the commissary sergeant, his wife and five children.

Eliza conducted children's Bible class with the help of three ladies, but the weather kept one such December class down to three blacks, two Indians and an unspecified number of white children. Eliza didn't fare as well during the church service, though, becoming ill from a combination of an overheating stove and tobacco smells. She recovered and went to the evening service. She was able to conduct her adult art class, though. Eliza also was suffering from headaches and what she thought was arthritis (or bursitis) in her shoulder and arm again, taking a quinine pill.

One of the holiday parties the Dodds attended was the cavalry ball, where everyone mixed and danced together; this must have been a treat for the enlisted men to dance with the ladies of Officers Row.

An impromptu party was held at an officer's home to try out their new coffee roaster, and that wife had fun making coffee for all. Perhaps a little brandy was added to help counter the caffeine's effects.

Now Eliza began preparing for the children's Christmas party, although some of her time was taken up with Amzi's new dog. She had to make sure it was indoors on the day when stray dogs were to be shot. Unfortunately, when their party occurred, some children were still sick from a vaccination, presumably for smallpox, but the ladies served candies, ice cream, nuts, raisins, cut tongue and buttered biscuits.

Of course Santa showed up with presents for all. Her last entry for Christmas Eve read, "and it's the night before Christmas and not a creature is stirring except myself."

January of 1882 rolled around and she noted that "Old Mother Shipton[']s" prediction that the world would end at the strike of 12:01 A.M. had passed.

The Christmas Day children's Bible class was without a single child, because all had received ice skates, and the ice was great. So the Dodds went to them and conducted an outdoor class. They sang songs, had a Bible lesson, and sang the Lord's Prayer, before the couple gave them cards and individual bags of cake, raisins and nuts. The Dodds attended an evening party at the McCulloh home, which featured a midnight supper of turkey, oysters, chicken and all the trimmings. Eliza especially enjoyed the tour of the house.

Eliza herself cooked a variety of meals, such as fish balls or shrimp pudding for breakfast, and steak and eggs for lunch, or toast and hash for breakfast and conventional fried chicken for lunch, or steak and fried potatoes for breakfast, then oyster croquettes and Saratoga potatoes for lunch. Supper was very light. January of 1882 was a good month for officer promotions, but not for dealing with servants. Officers Henry Black, Richard Morris, G.N. Bomford, and a "Wheeler" received promotions, with Black becoming a full colonel and moving on, while Morris became a major, assuming the post commander position. Black succeeded Ruger when he became the Montana District leader in Helena. Black's leaving didn't affect the women's hierarchy since he either wasn't married or his wife wasn't with him. Servant-wise, Eliza's couple were feuding again, apparently when he drank in excess, and Mrs. Norwood's black servants ran away. Eliza also mentioned cleaning the parlor herself, which "takes nearly all the morning."

In February she started recording the daily egg counts. Her first entry stated "5 eggs today" and "getting deaf." For an apparent ear infection she used "sweet oil." In addition, Mrs. Wheeler was carried out of the church service during the last song with a side ache, and Eliza was still having hearing problems. But Eliza's duties went on—cleaning, killing chickens to cook, etc. She did find a new book, *My Love*, to dive into, but more sick people needed some of her attention.

Although there were smallpox vaccinations, there was no defense against diseases such as typhoid fever, measles, diphtheria, whooping cough, cholera, tuberculosis, influenza, Rocky Mountain fever, and so on. The mortality rate of mothers and infants was considerable because of the high number of pregnancies, and minimal prenatal care. Antiseptics and anesthesia were not always used, either. Medical science finally began to move out of the Dark Ages when bona fide medical schools were established at a handful of eastern colleges. Many doctors still trained via the apprentice system, though.

Eliza's diary moved on from diseases to news of troops being sent out. Rarely had winter expeditions been needed since Sitting Bull and his people had settled on Dakota Territory reservations.

But these troops went east to rescue Chouteau County Sheriff John Healy and his deputy, Alfred Hamilton. These two had started the wave of whiskey forts in Canada with the establishment of Fort Hamilton, also called Fort Whoop-Up. Once the Northwest Mounted Police arrived, Healy went legitimate, operating the *Fort Benton Record* and serving as sheriff. The cavalry rescued Healy from a contingent of Métis and Plains Cree, who would not allow him to confiscate their illegally obtained furs.

Eliza mainly worried about the troops' suffering on this intensely cold, 150-mile trip while sleeping in tents, and she hoped that the lawmen would not be "scalped" before the army arrived.

That evening, after visiting with Mrs. Benham, Barnhart and Miller, she saw a "splendid meteor" that passed overhead and lit up the whole parade grounds. At first she thought the area was on fire. Emanating from it, she saw what looked like red and blue balls. The body was a bright yellow with a long, white tail. Few saw it, she said, because it happened just after lights out.

She especially enjoyed the social at Mrs. Miller's because of seeing her first example of static electricity. Lieutenant Thomas McClare rubbed Stephen's coat with a fur cap, then placed his finger near Stephen's nose so that a spark jumped and they heard a snap.

The number of servants shrank again when the Potter's Chinese servant hanged himself in the cellar. Mrs. Potter found him there in the morning. Meanwhile Eliza's servant Higgins was abusing his wife again because of his continuous drinking. He was threatening to leave, but would Mary?

Next there was an epidemic of chimney fires, first the Dodds', then the O'Briens', Klines' and Baldwins'. Eliza also had some unexpected visitors: Mrs. Anderson, Mrs. Barnhart, and their children, when a powerful windstorm developed and they sought shelter.

The small, but personally meaningful, passages of life continued, some cherished, some endured: rounds of informal and formal social affairs, church services and Bible classes, art classes and impromptu songfests, constant food preparations, local shopping and mail ordering, walks and buggy rides, letters sent and received, making and repairing clothing, egg and chicken work, buying milk tickets and grouse varieties from "the bandman" and, yes, constant illnesses and losing friends to rotation or death.

The warmer weather brought life as egg production increased, and Eliza allowed some to hatch. The March and April windstorms hammered the fort and brought down the commissary roof. During one storm, Eliza feared that the windows would blow in. The chickens suffered too, with one saved when it blew into the swill barrel and almost drowned. However, between gusts, outdoor walks resumed, the post garden was plowed, and flowers were planted.

Some not-so-ordinary news involved the post commander, Richard Morris. He was not well, and the doctors at St. Clare Hospital in Fort Benton could do nothing for his "head trouble." He was having spells of "being crazy," even attacking his attendants. Sometimes it took four to five men to restrain him. This could have been a recurrence of syphilis, a fatal illness that went into remission for years, and returned with a vengeance, attacking the body's organs, tissues and central nervous system. Major Jacob Kline was now in command. As an ironic footnote, the Morris family's chicken eggs spoiled without hatching. "Major Morris is quite insane, has no lucid movements now" was her next entry, followed by recording his death.

She and Stephen continued to enjoy the new spring; she loved the "beauty of the wilds." A picnic and fishing trip to the mountains was organized in spite of her worsening back problems. Stephen became ill afterwards, worried he had contracted the Rocky Mountain fever, but he recovered. (It would be discovered years later that the deadly malady was transmitted by wood ticks.)

Two of their friends were leaving, the Barnhart and Anderson families with Ella and Kate. She noted her sadness to see their apartments empty.

Good news came in the form of their apartment's being painted, but following that came threatening news: The steamboat

General Meade arrived at Coal Banks Landing carrying smallpox, and all Fort Assinniboine residents had to be vaccinated. Eliza also developed a boil on her rear end, both painful and dangerous from an infection standpoint. There was no sitting in church for a while.

Their egg and chicken industry received a boost because the carpenters began building the women a cooperative chicken coop.

At the end of May, the funeral service was held for Major Morris. On the first of June, Eliza planted flowers and the carpenters put up the window screens; plus she and Stephen picnicked at the wood camp in Beaver Creek valley.

She noted on June 23 that it had been one year since she had been home to Ohio.

She received a new dress via mail, but it was so homely she gave it to Julia Smith, age thirteen, daughter of laundress Tressa Smith. Servant Higgins had kept his promise and left. Mary was spending more time at the Benhams', and finally decided to change employer, hence their cook was gone, too. Amzi had his meals at the restaurant to ease his mother's new burden. Julia Smith began helping out while Amzi wrote to an employment agency for a replacement. The perceived servant-stealing was condemned by Eliza's circle of friends, who tried to help out by lending their own servants.

She mentioned that the McCulloh family suffered an ordeal when "old Mrs. McCulloh" was thrown onto the wheels of their carriages. Further, Mrs. Kellogg had hysterics when she witnessed it. Accidents were as much feared as disease.

Come fall, she mentioned that the three summer female guests had departed. Their visits were considered shopping trips for the young women hoping to find young officer husbands.

Eliza, although not well, joined the other women to activate the social circle once all the officers returned from summer field duty. She noticed that Mrs. Elizabeth McCulloh took a fall and "hurt her body," which resulted in some paralysis. Then Mrs. Wheeler became quite ill, and Mr. Cabenis had his toes frozen on a visit to

Fort Benton. Now the circle kicked in with visits and food. For her own leisure, one night Eliza read a novel until 2:00 A.M. She and Stephen attended a reception for the new commander, Lt. Colonel Guido Ilges, at the home of Major and Mrs. Kellogg. Now two more women fell sick, and Stephen had another apparent eye infection, hence they received food gifts.

The McCollohs left for Helena to put his mother, and perhaps a niece, on a train. The elder Mrs. McCulloh died the following year in Missouri.

Into March, Stephen's eye was still bad enough that sunlight hurt it, and Eliza was too sick to cook, but three days later she taught her art class. The following day she baked and returned to the visiting circuit.

In mid-March, she wrote that Laura Shannon wasn't able to clean her house today because her mother Dora was ill after the baby's birth. She visited Mrs. Shannon with Mrs. Norwood. She wrote, "She looked badly—was trembling all over—She is very ill." Dr. Craighill stayed with her until her death later that night. The baby died a week later. Dora Shannon had been a laundress at the fort. Besides Laura, age thirteen, she had a younger son and daughter, Willie and Mary. (A Private M. Shannon was listed in the 2nd Cavalry roll.) Mother and infant were buried in the fort cemetery. Then another round of sickness struck the women's circle. Perhaps Molly Shannon's illness had been passed on. A Mrs. Harwood was diagnosed with Bright's disease, which is an inflammation of the kidneys. She may have been the wife of the fort's guide.

Spring had come, and the troops moved out to their summer camps in northern Montana, where hot spots of violence and thievery were located. Eliza had her own troubles: someone was stealing the eggs, and Stephen was down with a dose of dysentery, but he cured it with "lots of Brandy." The circle baked goods for the officers to take out to their camps. Eliza was subsequently upset when soldiers chased away the Indians who were working at Broadwater's Landing wood camp, instead of chasing the horse-thief raiders from Canada. She mentioned several patrol actions that occurred.

The job-contracting company found her a new servant, or she inherited him when a couple left. Easter went well for both the Dodds, and Stephen celebrated another birthday. Eliza was corresponding with the wives who had moved with their husbands to other assignments, as well as writing to her own family and other friends. She added a new wrinkle to chicken raising and egg production: they now had turkeys. Unfortunately some would be stolen on July Fourth, and she suspected the bachelor officers.

A cold May 8 was a bad day for her. She wrote of a painful attack of rheumatism in her neck, back and arm. For several days she couldn't sit up. In the midst of this, her apparent best friends, the Norwoods, were gone. The other wives gave the Dodds help with their servants. It took three weeks before Eliza got out socializing in stylish tight, long-sleeved dresses, but she went for only a short duration, and then returned home and put on a loose calico dress. She later noted a prickly feeling in the hand of her bad arm. The doctor gave her a liniment to soothe the pain and limit crippling effects.

In spite of this, she tried to function, doing limited visitation, directing Sunday school, and supervising the chicken coop with Stephen's help. By the beginning of June she felt somewhat better, although cold, windy weather didn't help. Egg production continued to rise; she gave the bachelor officers several gifts of fresh eggs.

She wrote on June 6 that the old brown hen hatched seven turkey eggs. The weather continued unpleasant, and a picnic was canceled. On June 9, Eliza remembered the birthday of her sister Lollie, apparently her favorite. Eliza started working on a new dress, and made pies. She didn't mention any further health problems until late June. The cold, rainy, windy weather stopped for a few days, allowing a few very warm days.

July 4 was her last major entry. She slept through early morning reveille when the band played "Yankee Doodle Dandy," "Hail Columbia," and "The Star Spangled Banner." She did hear gunfire thirty-eight times at noon, however, and enjoyed the fireworks while flying a kite with Mrs. Hoyt. From July 15, her diary skipped to August 6 and then to October 9, 1883. She ended with a snow report and how it had snowed on the 10th when she started her diary two years previously. Eliza's last notation was, "My dress came last night. Stephen got pants."

We have no further personal information about her. Thanks to Loy Chvilicek, we learn that Eliza and Stephen took a leave, returning home for Thanksgiving and Christmas of 1884. They are both mentioned in the Fort Benton newspaper departing on a riverboat, but only his name appears as returning to Fort Benton and Fort Assinniboine. Stephen also took a later week's leave in October of 1885. One could only wonder if Eliza had remained temporarily in the East with serious health problems, but she returned in 1885.

Stephen retired from the army in 1890. The couple moved to Boise, where he again became a civilian minister. Amzi soon joined them. Following a familiar path, they next returned to Salt Lake City. Eliza traveled to Boise in 1895 to meet Amzi's soon-to-be bride, Anna Laura Whitlock, and died there of a heart attack. Her body was not sent home to Ohio, instead being buried in Boise's Morris Hill Cemetery. Stephen remained until he moved to San Diego in 1911, where he is buried in Fort Rosecrans' National Cemetery on the Pacific Ocean. Amzi died in 1932 in Ventura city or county.

There is irony in that such a close-knit family is not buried together.

These "fragile and refined" women perhaps had no permanent affect on the Milk River Country, since they were gone before the Gros Ventre–Assiniboine Reservation was pushed back to allow Anglo settlement. Yet they are an important part of our western history. Eliza in particular receives credit for setting both a humane and religious tone for the ladies of the regiments and others at the "Fortress on the Plains."

Métis Prince of the Plains
Gabriel Dumont, 1837-1906

A DUST-COVERED RIDER—probably from the Fort Belknap Indian Reservation—pulled up in front of another fort's headquarters on a hard-ridden, sweat-covered horse. He dashed inside, Fort Assinniboine guards just behind him because he didn't stop at the gate. Catching his breath, the rider reported that Gabriel Dumont, the wanted military leader of the failed North West Rebellion in Saskatchewan, had been seen. His last location, he said, was traveling south down Clear Creek, ten or so miles northwest of the fort, and further that he had another male rider with him. The date was May 26, 1885.

Gabriel Dumont. RCMP HERITAGE CENTER ARCHIVES, REGINA, SK, CANADA

The commander presumably promised the man a reward if Dumont was captured, and ordered out a detachment of 1st Cavalry troops under a Sergeant Perkins. They easily captured the "Canadian rebel," since neither Dumont or Michel Dumas was making any effort to conceal himself. In fact, Dumont wanted to see the fort's doctor to attend to his bullet-grazed forehead.

The twosome had eluded capture by a Canadian militia

force eleven days earlier after the rebellion's final battle, at Batoche, a village on the South Saskatchewan River. The normally 275-mile trip took them 600 miles by night, as the pair detoured around Saskatoon, and crossed the Saskatchewan's southerly elbow, where Lake Diefenbaker is now located. From there they traveled southwest into the Battle Creek Valley of the Cypress Hills. They followed the creek into Montana, crossed the Milk River near present-day Lohman—then a trading post—and started down Clear Creek. Throughout the trip, the two were helped by Métis and Indian people.

At the time, Dumont was about forty-eight years of age, and described as a man of medium height with heavy shoulders and head. His face sported a scraggly beard and mustache with unkempt long hair, but a battle campaign didn't make for careful grooming. His trunk was more slender, yet compact from his life as an all around outdoorsman and veteran horseman. Author-historian Joseph Kinsey Howard described his face as, "...open and kindly, almost childishly innocent." However, this was deceptive since it easily turned to anger and subsequent viciousness when the established Métis rules and regulations were not followed. "Métis," from a French term for mixed blood, referred usually to Cree or Chippewa blood combined with that of French or Scotch traders. The separatist Métis society was based on farming, trapping, and a strong community spirit rooted in Native and French Catholic traditions.

As a young man, in the 1870s, Dumont showed natural leadership that commanded such respect that he was invited to captain the two Saskatchewan annual buffalo hunts, which operated under a rigorous military discipline, with pomp and majesty as the men traveled in their colorful, beaded outfits of Anglo-Saxon, French and Chippewa-Cree designs. Accompanying the hunt were as many as a thousand people in a thousand one-ox Red River carts.

When Gabriel was a child, these hunts originated from Métis homes at St. Boniface, Manitoba, and the Pembina–St. Joseph area of North Dakota, and traveled across the plains of the Dakotas, Montana and Saskatchewan. This brought them into conflict with Indian tribes, especially the three branches of the Sioux Nation. The Métis, with their superior firepower and military discipline and tactics, rarely lost a battle.

During the first Métis Rebellion in Manitoba, in 1869, this clan of Dumont's moved west, following the diminishing buffalo herds and seeking a new homeland beyond the wave of settlers. They found this in a north-central area of Saskatchewan, along the north and south branches of the Saskatchewan River between Saskatoon and Prince Albert. Other groups settled at Spring Creek (Lewistown) and along the Milk River in Montana.

Dumont by the age of ten performed the usual required camp duties; one day, while making smudge fires to ward away mosquitoes, he heard what he thought was a Sioux attack and rushed to his father demanding a rifle to fight them. It turned out it was only buffalo, but that day he graduated from the bow and arrow to the rifle. Dumont's talents went beyond the usual Métis expertise, including swimming and the age-old Sarcee Indian trick of being able to call buffalo to his location during a hunt. Dumont could speak several Indian languages and French, but could not speak English well, nor could he read or write it.

Dumont settled on a river site a few miles south of Batoche. There he operated a river ferry service on a shortcut road to Fort Carleton, the Hudson's Bay Company (H.B.C.) post. He farmed and operated his own small trading store. Dumont prided himself in having the only billiards table in that part of the country.

The French-Indian peoples moved their unofficial capital from St. Laurent to the village of Batoche on the Saskatchewan River in about 1873. Thanks to such business people as Xavier "Batoche" Letendre, it became one of the most successful commercial centers in the North West Territories. Dumont became their leader with eight councilors elected under him, including his brother and cousin. The nucleus of their laws originated from the precise old rules under which their buffalo hunts operated. Also, the mainly Roman Catholic Métis took direction from the priests of the St. Anthony Church on the hill above the town. Usually a priest went along on the hunts.

The Canadian government would not recognize their government, as had the French, or anyone else's land rights, until a complete survey was done. The three territorial districts of the North West Territories didn't have a representative in Parliament, although they were supposedly represented at the Territorial Council meetings in Regina. The government had already signed treaties with the various Indian tribes to allow the railroad through, followed by a soon-to-be influx of settlers.

All the petitions of the Anglo-Saxon and Scotch Métis peoples had been ignored for the last eleven years. When the territorial surveys did begin, the Métis saw its being done in conventional squares, and not by their traditional river-lot system. Again the Métis saw themselves with their backs against the wall, anticipating that their culture and language were beginning the same disappearing act that had happened to tribes in eastern Canada.

In the interim, Dumont's word was law throughout the Saskatchewan River country. He punished all people for violating their law of the land with fines, beatings, and property seizure. This brought him into conflict with the North West Mounted Police when he arrested, and seized the carts, horses and supplies of, a Hudson's Bay Company hunting party of forty men.

The powerful H.B.C., which earlier sold its English charter of lands to the Dominion of Canada—in the are now called the North West Territories—complained to the Mounted Police via their factor at Fort Carleton, located just nineteen miles west of Batoche. Until that incident, the Mounted Police thought the distinctive Métis organization was a good thing, but now they might be becoming too militant—and needed to be watched.

Finally the Métis leaders decided more direct action had to be taken, hence Louis Riel was to be summoned from Montana. The mainly Scotch Riel had been the leader of the Métis Rebellion in 1869-1870, when they seized H.B.C. Fort Garry (future Winnipeg), declaring themselves a new nation. Former New France was now British North America, meaning they had lost all rights claimed under the French. After ten months, the government seized the post, although the Métis had vacated it. Shortly after the Manitoba Act was passed, it gave Métis land and citizenship equal to Natives' rights. The government also gave supposed immunity to the rebel Métis, although the leaders were banished or subjected to trial for the death of a British citizen during their seizures.

Riel had become a Montana citizen, working such jobs at the river port of Carroll on the Missouri River as woodchopper, sub-agent for a trading company, and representative-agent for the Métis peoples. He also did part-time clerical-legal work at the Chouteau County Courthouse, and finally taught at the Jesuit-run St. Peter's Mission School west of present-day Cascade between Great Falls and Helena on the Missouri River. He now had a wife and child, but he still dreamed of the Métis people's having their own nation within a nation. The priests thought his religious and political views were on the radical side, but the children loved him.

Riel accepted, although he felt he could do little, but the Canadian government did owe him for his own grievances, he believed. So Riel, with his family, left for Canada. At Fort Benton, he received the blessing of Father Frederick H. Eberschweiler, a pioneer Montana Jesuit from Germany. Along with the blessing came the admonition not to start a war with the Canadian government, because although he might win several battles, he would have fewer men left in the end to fight the larger force. Riel claimed it would be a peaceful protest.

But the priest was worried, especially since he knew that Riel had been listening to Fort Benton members of the anti-Canadian Fenian movement, which was a 19th-century secret organization of Irish immigrants and Irish-Americans dedicated to the violent overthrow of the British government in Ireland.

When Riel arrived in the Saskatchewan River country accompanied by a party under Dumont, he met with many enthusiastic

Scotch and French Métis and Anglo Saxon people who were afraid of losing their property rights once the country opened to settlement. Inspired by this welcome, Riel got right to his legal work, and began sending petitions to Ottawa that went unanswered, although the Mounted Police urged political action before violence erupted. A federal government investigating committee was being formed, but the petitioning people were either uninformed of it, or didn't believe the news.

Some of his regional supporters became concerned as Riel's mission took on an almost Messianic tone while Riel's mental state seemed to deteriorate and his actions became at times irrational, aggressive and militant.

Finally Riel decided to get the attention of the government by again establishing a Provisional Government of Saskatchewan as he had in Manitoba, only this time he was on Canadian government land, not private H.B.C. lands, so he was now leading an insurrection. Perhaps this is what he meant when he told the Fort Benton priest he saw himself swinging from a gallows.

The first spark of battle happened when the Mounted Police began bringing additional men to fortify Fort Carlton. Then the H.B.C. factor, Malcolm Clarke, told some Métis freighters that 500 more police were coming to Saskatchewan to arrest Riel and the council members. Because of this report, the Métis declared war, with Dumont as their military leader. Riel considered this only as a "demonstration," not a war, but he scared off the Anglo-Saxon and Scotch Métis, leaving only some of the French Métis, numbering 500 fighters on a good day. Riel also alienated the Roman Catholic Church, which believed in peaceful methods such as Riel had originally used. The local priests called him the "anti-Christ," because he began calling himself a prophet, higher than the Church and answering only to God.

Dumont immediately put his force together, and struck the first blows, seizing the guns, ammunition and supplies from the two village stores. That night he sent out riders to cut the telegraph lines to the outside world, and watch all trails. Next Dumont would lead his forces to the adjacent community of Duck Lake to seize supplies from their store.

Major Crozier of the Mounted Police detachment, now at the H.B.C. post of Fort Carlton, sent envoys to Riel, trying to negotiate the return of the Duck Lake goods and the release of prisoners. Riel refused, and instead demanded the Mounted Police vacate the trading post. Crozier refused and requested NWMP reinforcements from Regina. He decided to act before the additional men arrived, and started for Duck Lake with fifty-six police, forty-three volunteers from Prince Albert, a caravan, and sleds to bring back the supplies.

Dumont's infantry forces lay in ambush for the Mounted Police on a low hill above the Duck Lake trail, concealed behind brush or dirt mounds. Dumont and others on horseback waited in an adjacent coulee. However, in spite of poor visibility and snow, Crozier's advance scouts spotted the Métis, hence they halted and formed a line across the trail with their twenty sleds.

Isidore Dumont and native fighter Chief Aseeweyin rode forward to parley with Major Crozier and his English-Métis interpreter, John McKay. The discussion never got started because Dumont's companion grabbed for McKay's rifle, and McKay opened fire. Crozier then raced back to his lines and gave the order to fire. After a half hour of fighting, three Mounted Police and nine volunteers had died, with eleven wounded. The Métis lost five men, including Gabriel's brother, and three wounded, one being Gabriel who had stood in front of his troops. Crozier saw that they were almost surrounded, and he ordered a retreat. The rebels wanted to pursue them, but Riel had seen enough violence and countermanded Edouard and Gabriel Dumont's orders to follow them. The insurgents did secure a dozen rifles, eight horses and five sleds, but not the cannon, which would have been invaluable in coming battles.

This would be a constant problem for Dumont: Riel interfering in his battle plans. Dumont felt he could win using guerrilla tactics, while Riel only wanted to make a stand to show strength sufficient to convince the government it must deal honorably with the Métis. Apparently Riel did not understand that, whether he caused one death or several, it was still an armed insurrection against the Dominion of Canada.

The "Mountie" reinforcements arrived the next day, but they decided the trading post wasn't defensible and torched it before retreating to Prince Albert. Dumont knew a perfect place to ambush them but Riel said no; they wouldn't fight like Indians.

In response to what the governments of Canada and the United States thought could be a major uprising, especially with native help, Ottawa sent the Northwest Field Force, composed of two divisions. The First Division of about 900 men under Major General Frederick Middleton arrived at the end of the tracks at Fort Qu'Appelle, and Middleton established a base camp a few miles to the north. Now they would begin a 200-mile trek north to Batoche in harsh winter conditions to face a few hundred Métis. Two units of the Second Division arrived to contend with two Plains Cree tribes who joined the rebels, one causing trouble in the Fort Pitt–Frog Lake area and another in the Battleford area. Troops from Fort Assinniboine were positioned on the U.S. border, along with Canadian volunteers on the opposite side, but no Indian or Métis people in Montana wanted to be involved, in spite of Riel's attempts, at least until they saw who was winning.

Dumont, of course, had spies watching the clumsy, uncoordinated advance, and he concocted a plan to rain havoc on them by dynamiting the Canadian Pacific railroad track and bridges, attacking the lightly guarded prairie posts containing food and hay for horses, and conducting nightly raids on the poorly located and defended base camp. Dumont said, "I could have made them so edgy that at the end of three nights they would have been at each other's throats." Riel again said no; he still hoped that their smaller operations would not be considered a war and that peace was still possible. Dumont continued the debate, but Riel would not back down, and Dumont obeyed like a good soldier, as soldiers had to do to with politicians.

Middleton's unobstructed force continued north under the watch of the frustrated Métis fighters. His militia was now forty-five miles from Batoche, on the South Saskatchewan River at Clark's Crossing. There they were to have met the steamer *Northcote* with additional supplies, but it was late; also at that point Middleton divided his force into two columns, sending them along each side of the river for a two-prong attack against Batoche.

Dumont, in the interim, knew he couldn't fight such great odds and superior firepower once the soldiers were at the village, and he told Riel he must attack now. Riel finally agreed reluctantly. He had to keep some of his force at the village because Mounted Police scouts from Prince Albert had been seen in the area, perhaps a prelude to an attack. The splitting of the Canadian militia gave them a chance to fight a smaller unit, since the ice-clogged river would not be easy for the other part of the unit to re-cross.

Dumont set up his ambush for one of the columns with his 150 men, five miles north near a stream called Fish Creek in the large Tourand's Coulee that Middleton had to cross. To close the trap, Dumont led twenty mounted men in a coulee to the south. However, they lost the element of surprise when the advance scouts discovered fresh tracks and recent campfire sites. The mounted Métis force ran into an ambush and lost two men. They safely retreated, with Dumont covering them from behind a thicket. Upon his return to the ravine crest, he found that some of the men had deserted after hearing the gunfire. The main battle lasted about twelve hours. The Battle of Fish Creek started at 7:30 A.M. on the 24th of April, about one month since the first battle with the Mounted Police near Duck Lake.

The battle went well for the Métis since they still held the high ground against the troops in the coulee. Dumont's tactic of moving troops around convinced Middleton that he was up against 300 men, although there were only 62 after the casualties, desertions or absences of messengers going back and forth to Batoche. The muzzle-loading shotguns did their best work at this range, firing pieces of jagged metal, lead or broken horseshoe nails.

The Métis were actually enjoying themselves against the green recruits, as they sang songs with flute accompaniment. Brief sunshine brought praise of the first yellow and purple blooms of spring wildflowers. Dumont joked that the enemies' bullets wouldn't hurt them as he casually picked off a young Canadian officer and laughed as he heard his sounds of dying. They also cheered when Edouard Dumont arrived with reinforcements. The fun ended when the army withdrew just after dark. The militia counted ten killed and forty wounded. (Another casualty was Middleton's fur cap that Dumont put a bullet through.) The Métis lost six, with two wounded. Their real loss, however, was fifty horses killed. Dumont and his cadre celebrated, in the rain, with a brandy toast courtesy of an officer's abandoned medical kit, though Dumont verbally credited Riel and the women at the village for praying for them from dawn to dusk.

Middleton's second column finally re-crossed the river, and the unit camped on the river for several days, waiting for supplies by riverboat and sending the wounded back. Once these things were accomplished, the troops moved on to Gabriel's Crossing, where they exacted revenge. They used lumber from Riel's buildings to reinforce the decks of the *Northcote* and torched the rest. Middleton intended to use the steamer now as a gunboat, to create a river diversion at Batoche while his main force attacked the village overland from the south. Gabriel shrugged off the loss, except the theft of his wife's pedal-powered washing machine and his billiard table. The militia men also helped themselves to souvenirs in the other mostly vacated homes.

The Métis and Indian allies—small groups of Plains Cree, Chippewa, Assiniboine and Santee Sioux under Chief White Cap—won two battles, but their ammunition was mostly expended and their fields barren from no farming. Their larders were empty and they had no time to hunt, yet some people did break Riel and Dumont's commands not to feed the priests. The clergy were out of favor because they continued to tell the masses that their leaders were wrong in their rebellion against the government. Dumont had little time to worry about the Fathers. He had to ready the village for the full force of Middleton's soldiers, cannon and Gatling gun. The defenders dug rifle pits and trenches south and east of Batoche, most of these fortified with logs and camouflaged with earth, rocks and tree limbs. The defense was set up so Dumont could communicate all the way to the upper defenders just below Mission Ridge.

Earlier on, Riel had attempted to bring in Indian people from both sides of the border, telling them that all their grievances would be addressed if they joined the cause. Only two Cree bands, that of Poundmaker near Battleford, and Big Bear's band under Little Bear, Wandering Spirit and other sub-chiefs of the Fort Pitt–Frog Lake area, responded with a mix of Cree, Chippewa and Assiniboine. The Montana Métis peoples wanted nothing to do with it, and the other Canadian tribes listened to the Mounted Police, not Riel. The two Plains Cree bands that had responded fought only locally and were captured by the other two Canadian forces. Later it was learned that other Métis fighters were on they way after hearing of the Duck Lake battle, but they were too late.

Hence no help would come. The Batoche area Métis force of about two hundred were on their own, and defeat seemed inevitable.

The Canadians launched their two-pronged attack, with the *Northcote* sailing toward Batoche and the troops marching overland. The riverboat would open fire when the troops arrived on the morning of May 9. But military strategist Gabriel Dumont gave them a surprise: the boat was attacked from both sides of the river where it was at its narrowest. Dumont led the charge after shooting up the boat, but their attack failed because the boat's crew opened fire with the Gatling gun, enabling them to regain control of the pilot-less craft. Dumont then launched part two of his plan by loosening the ferry's cables to stop the craft. The first cable fell too late and the second only raked the top of the boat's superstructure. Major Boulton, chief of the scouts, tried to convince the ferry crew to return to the village, but they said no, we are not a warship; besides, the downed cables prevented it.

Thus Dumont was stopped from obtaining the ammunition and other supplies aboard the boat and two towed barges, and wasted more ammunition in the process. The "fun" was over and Middleton wasn't happy about the loss of the boat. The retired British officer really didn't want to confront the wily fox again, particularly without the planned two-pronged attack.

The Canadian militia force finally reached the top of the hill looking down on the village and the river, although no defenders were seen. There were the Church of St. Anthony, the parish house, with the cemetery and some cabins across the road. In front were lines of brush that extended all the way to the village. The soldiers opened fire across the field with the Gatling gun, causing several women and children to run into the brush towards the village. They then directed the cannon to fire on the village.

About the same time, according to Dumont and others on both sides, the priests met with Middleton and his staff; they conveyed that the Métis suffered from the lack of food and ammunition—and were small in numbers. Also the priests continued their attempts to save the defenders' lives (and souls) during the battle, even though they were considered traitors to the rebel cause.

The soldiers advanced until they were perfect silhouettes, and they were met with a wall of fire. In their hasty retreat, one cannon was almost abandoned because of being stuck in some brush; however, the automatic weapon covered its recovery.

The Métis, they discovered, had a series of pits and fox holes all the way to the river. Only at battle's end after four days did they see a Métis fighter. Dumont continued his bag of tricks, such as firing the prairie when the wind was right, and making feints at attacking their lines. That night the army retired behind an improvised stockade along with the horses, only to have the Métis lob missiles, yell insults or fire sporadically into the camp. This kept the horses nervous enough to bolt, so no one got any sleep. They ended the nerve-war tactics with a large rocket flare that burst over the camp.

The following day the cannon continued its destruction of the village, but couldn't be brought low enough to hit the Métis positions. Middleton tried no more advances, instead having the troops dig in and the artillery fire continued all day, with occasional bursts from the multi-barreled automatic gun. Dumont and Riel continued to encourage their men, sending messages up the hill's chain of fortified positions, while Riel circulated among the men in the pits, carrying his large cross.

Finally the army retreated back to the stockade area about 6:00 P.M., after the Métis feinted a charge when the sun was in the militia's eyes. The troops slept better that night with earthworks and behind further fortifications finished after the supply wagons arrived. Now two days had passed, and the battle was a draw so far because of the Gatling gun. Middleton believed Dumont had more than 200 fighters because of the Métis leader's constantly shifting warrior positions.

Unfortunately Dumont couldn't change his dire food situation. What little remained was given to the families hiding in the dug coulees along the riverbanks. Indian hunters scoured the countryside for stray cattle to bring them.

Day three came and went with the same results. Finally Middleton's officers convinced him to try more aggressive tactics. That fourth day, May 12, Riel predicted that if on the day they would survive this battle, the skies would be clear; on the other hand, if it were cloudy they would lose.

Middleton started the day with a flanking movement, as the main force struck straight ahead. It didn't work because the flankers didn't lay down the heavy cannon and Gatling gun as promised. However, Dumont did strengthen his own flank because of the aborted activity.

Twice during the battle, Riel threatened to kill their prisoners if any harm came to Indian families. These notes were used against him in his later trial, and it showed that the Métis knew their fate.

Middleton next allowed the Midland Battalion to advance cautiously for intelligence gathering. Instead, they charged and the other units followed, giving Middleton no choice but to call the reserves into the fight. The exhausted, starving, out-gunned and outnumbered Métis forces crumbled.

At that point, about 3:00 P.M., the sky darkened and the sun disappeared behind the clouds—they had offended God, Riel exclaimed.

The military seized the town, released the prisoners in the basement of Xavier "Batoche" Letendre's two-and-a-half story mansion, and gathered in the people hiding in the coulees and riverbank caves. Several patrols were sent out to find Riel, Dumont and other escapees. The captured Métis had to turn in their weapons, leaving nothing for them to hunt with.

In the meantime, the dead Métis fighters were buried in a mass grave, except 93-year-old Joseph Ouellette, for whom Father Vidal Fourmond found a coffin.

While searching for Riel, Gabriel and Madeline Dumont ministered to the children with some food, clothing and blankets. They found Marguerite Riel and the couple's two children, but no Louis. The couple left two blankets for her, as they moved on with their searches and assistance. Gabriel stopped to make moccasins from cowhide for some barefoot children.

Dumont made camp at night in the Birch Hills and spent three days looking for Riel. He kept them on the move until they reached his father's home. Here they would be safe because Isidore hadn't participated in the war, and he wasn't known to the army. Dumont received an invitation through other Métis to surrender and he replied, "You can say to Middleton that I am in the woods and I still have ninety bullets to use on his soldiers." Isidore convinced Dumont he must leave, and Madeline would be safe until he could later take her to Montana. Michel Dumas accompanied him on the trip to bring Riel from Montana.

At Fort Assinniboine the now-legendary Dumont intrigued the officers and men with his stories of the battles with the Mounted Police. He claimed to have put the hole in General Middleton's hat at the Battle of Batoche. The men made him prove his shooting by firing at a stone 800 yards distant on the firing range, which he hit.

Upon release as an official political refugee, he went to the Spring Creek (Lewistown) Métis settlement to devise an escape plan for Riel at the NWMP jail at Regina. He traveled all over Montana to recruit help and establish stations along the way. However, the Mounted Police got wind of it, and they strengthened the guard force.

Riel was executed in September of 1885, the dream of "new Catholic France" dying with him. His vision of dying by hanging came true.

Sadly, Gabriel Dumont's father died before they could be reunited. He was reunited with his family and wife, but she died of consumption after only a few months. Apparently he stayed at the Spring Creek colony, deciding what to do with his life now. Going "on the bum" didn't sit well with him, so he joined Buffalo Bill Cody's Wild West Show as the "Hero of the Half Breed Rebellion." He, of course, couldn't join them on their trip to Great Britain, where he was a wanted man.

From Montana, Dumont made many trips east on a lecture tour to address people sympathetic to the Métis cause. Since there was a general amnesty in effect, he was able to visit Saskatchewan and Quebec provinces to speak and raise awareness and funds for displaced French Métis. During that time he met up with two former adversaries, retired "Mountie" Major L.N.F. Crazier, and Lieutenant Arthur T. Howard of the Connecticut National Guard, master of the Gatling machine gun that destroyed the Métis. Howard claimed that he was always careful to aim above Dumont's head, but it is doubtful he ever saw the Métis leader during the battles. Howard was the man most hated by the Métis, with Prime Minister Sir John A. MacDonald a close second.

Eventually the interest in Dumont faded, for he no longer was a fugitive—the most wanted man—since the amnesty; also, the rough-cut Métis leader wasn't considered fit to represent the movement in eastern Canada. Along with the lecture circuit, coordinating with Joseph Riel (Louis's brother at Winnipeg), riding in the wild west show and seeking support in Paris, he spent time in Métis settlements and encampments, but it wasn't the same as in the old days. Gabriel finally returned to his old haunts in 1893, where relatives were farming his land. All he had to show for his efforts were a gold watch with chain, plus a silver medal given to him by the Métis people of New York. Dumont also obtained a strip of land under the Manitoba Land Act, which Riel had gained for them in 1870.

Gabriel settled in the nearby town of de Bellevue, and built a small log cabin on his grand–nephew Alex Dumont's farmland. He enjoyed years of hiking, fishing and hunting, riding, shooting, trapping and socializing with his many grandchildren and other relatives. He particularly enjoyed the celebrations, where he wore his suit with the medal and watch showing. A badge of courage was the scar on his forehead from the Duck Lake fight. He would let the children feel it and remarked, "You see, my skull was too thick for the English to kill me!"

He died in May of 1906, a few days after a hunting trip to nearby Baskin Lake. Dumont died in bed after consuming some soup. Old-time Father Julien Moulin conducted the funeral. Many Métis and Indian people came to it at Batoche, but the outside world had forgotten him after twenty-one years. But I'm sure his reunion with the nine Métis killed in the Battle of Batoche brought him a hearty welcome.

To quote the Gabriel Dumont Institute of Saskatoon, Saskatchewan, "Gabriel is remembered as a skillful leader of the Métis people in their struggles for responsible government and recognition of land claims."

Two Legendary Missionaries

Reverend Frederick H. Eberschweiler, S.J., 1839-1918

THIRTY-THREE-YEAR-OLD JESUIT Father Frederick Eberschweiler had a big decision to make in August of 1872: would he remain a member of the Roman Catholic Church's Jesuit religious order (Society of Jesus), move to another European country as his religious brothers did, leave the society in order to remain in his homeland of Rhineland, Germany, or leave Europe altogether and journey to Buffalo, New York, where other ousted Jesuits were reorganizing?

The newly formed German Empire under the Hohenzollern King Wilhelm I and Prince/Chancellor Otto von Bismarck, feared that the Church—especially the Jesuits—threatened the serenity of the new, largely Protestant nation. There had been years of military and political discord since the 16th century Protestant Reformation.

Eberschweiler had just com-

Father Eberschweiler. STUART C. MAC-KENZIE, CHINOOK, MT. GLASS NEG. PROCESSED BY MSU-N ARCHIVES, HAVRE

pleted three years of teaching German in a Jesuit school in France, and had returned, ill, when the Franco-Prussian War broke out. In the war, 1870-1871, German forces defeated the French under Emperor Napoleon III, and they occupied Paris for three years until a war indemnity of five billion francs was paid. The Jesuits, including Eberschweiler, acted as chaplains/nurses for both sides in the conflict.

It was after this war that the Jesuits received the ultimatum. But, since the priest had more interest in saving souls than in politics, he elected to go to America to pursue that goal.

For the next ten years he stayed in the eastern United States, working as a seminary teacher in Cleveland, Ohio, and an assistant church pastor in Toledo, Ohio, and Burlington, Iowa.

Next he joined in missionary work in the wilds of northern Montana. From the local Jesuit headquarters at St. Peter's Mission, near present-day Cascade on the stagecoach trail between the Sun River and the capital at Helena, Eberschweiler was assigned as the first resident priest at Fort Benton on the Missouri River. Before the railroads came, it was the most important inland river port, transportation and trading center in Montana from the 1860s to the 1890s. It was also briefly a military post before Fort Shaw was built on the Sun River.

Eberschweiler's new parish included a large portion of northeast and central Montana. In spite of the hundreds of miles he logged by foot, horseback, buggy or stagecoach, he remained a cheerful, tireless and optimistic man of God, always looking forward to the next worship service or baptism given in his German-accented English. But, he was also described as sad at heart, because of his fellow man's lack of interest in God and the Church.

He particularly enjoyed stage travel, which allowed him the companionship of riding up top with the driver. He rode the Benton stagecoach every second month to the military fort of Assinniboine, between the Bear's Paw Mountains and the Milk River, forty miles from the international border with the North West Territories of Canada. They left Fort Benton at 4:00 A.M. with stops at such places as Mose Solomon's trading post on the Marias River, and Big Sandy and Box Elder, before completing the seventy-some miles to the military post after dark. Future events at this fort would dramatically change the priest's life.

Through the military-post and civilian trading operation where the stage depot was located, Eberschweiler got to know employees Simon Pepin, E.T. Broadwater and L.K. Devlin. Pepin had been the wagon-master since Diamond R Transportation had begun freighting from Utah. Now his main job was as foreman of the cattle herds and slaughterhouse. Broadwater was a store clerk and bookkeeper, while Devlin, a former civilian supervisor of military stone masons, now helped manage the trading complex. All three would be prominent businessmen of Havre when it arose in the following decade.

At the store, the priest bought a journal to record baptisms, marriages and deaths until churches could be built.

He also became acquainted with the Gros Ventre (White Clay People) and Assiniboine (Nakoda, Yanktonai Sioux), who lived in the area and acted as scouts for the military.

Sporadically over the years, starting in 1846, Jesuits made trips to these and other tribes of northern Montana. Jesuit Father Giarda had a rather rough time in 1867 when Chief Bull Lodge's men took him prisoner and temporarily stripped him of his possessions and outer clothing in return for a blanket. However, he returned a few months later and received a warmer reception.

A delegation from the Fort Belknap Reservation asked Fr. Eberschweiler to establish a mission for them. The priest reported the request to both his Jesuit superior and the Bishop of Helena. After preliminary negotiations, he became the Indian missionary for both the Fort Belknap and the Fort Peck trading post/reservation areas. Fort Peck served Nakoda Sioux in addition to Assiniboine.

On his next trip to Fort Assinnibione, he took his few earthly possessions and portable altar. Colonel Elwell Otis personally welcomed and congratulated him on his new venture. Eberschweiler said he "...gave me such a hard shaking as I never got in my life. I found after it a five dollar gold piece in my hand! If all my handshaking were such ones…" Otis also provided dinner and an ambulance for his trip. The same year Otis helped feed Plains Cree who had fled from Alberta and Saskatchewan after the failure of the North West (Métis) Rebellion; they congregated around the fort on Beaver Creek. Otis later became military governor of the Philippines after the Spanish-American War.

The priest arrived at the Fort Belknap trading post/Indian agency, just south of present-day Chinook, and presented his official papers to Indian agent Major W.L. Lincoln. His reception was less than cordial. He next spoke to the Irish post trader Thomas O'Hanlon who, as a Catholic, was more receptive, and the trader made arrangements with some locals to erect a rudimentary log cabin for the priest's residence and chapel. It was located south of future Harlem on the Milk River near the present-day Fort Belknap agency.

The dirt-floored cabin contained two rooms, each fifteen by eighteen feet. In his report, Eberschweiler called it his "new cathedral," making it official by placing a large crucifix over the door. There on December 8, 1885, the missionary conducted his first Eucharist service for only O'Hanlon and one of his employees, along with several curious Indian people looking on. On the room's interior walls, Eberschweiler placed several colorful lithographs to attract them.

Eberschweiler was now about twenty-one miles from Fort Belknap and another twenty-five miles from Fort Assinniboine. He was truly isolated.

First on his list was learning the two Indian languages, thanks to agency interpreter Bill Bent. His father, William, had built the large trading post, Bent's Fort, on the Arkansas River in Colorado on the Santa Fe Trail. Bill Bent was the product of his father's marriage to a Cheyenne woman.

The site of the priest's chapel-home lacked decent water, lumber, fuel, and it was too far from the Indian settlements. Also, Eberschweiler wasn't happy with the "white degenerates" who hung around

Fort Belknap and Fort Assinniboine. In 1890, after conferring with his new converts, he set out with a guide to look over the country to the south near the Little Rocky Mountains. He founded a permanent mission site on Peoples Creek, just short of what would be called Mission Canyon. The missionary immediately wrote his Jesuit superior, Father Cataldo, of his successful trip, stating, "I only can compare that most beautiful country with the promised land where milk and honey flows." Eberschweiler went on to detail the plentiful grass for raising cattle, the abundant timber, good water and the rich soil for growing crops.

The new mission site, to be called St. Paul's, was included in the new permanent reservation ratified by Congress in May of 1888, which encompassed 840,000 acres of prairie and foothills from the Milk River to the Little Rocky Mountains. A new agency was set up on the Milk River near the priest's first cabin. Reportedly, Eberschweiler helped the two tribes deal with the Northwest Treaty Commission, and he wrote the initial thirty-page document that defined their land wants.

Now the transplanted Rhinelander's priority was building the mission. He went to Fort Benton to find workers and lumber, but found neither since no one would venture there after warfare had broken out between the local Gros Ventre and the Blackfoot Bloods of Alberta, Canada, southwest of Lethbridge.

A brief 1880s placer gold rush to the Little Rockies gave the missionary access to a volunteer manpower force he needed to build four log buildings under a man called Enstat. These buildings were initially a church/residence, convent and school. Tom O'Hanlon, his old friend from Fort Belknap, procured a thousand feet of finished lumber for floors, sashes and roofs. O'Hanlon was just three years from establishing the town site of Chinook.

Eberschweiler's rapid process of proselytizing the Gros Ventre and Upper Assiniboine led to his new assignment to the Milk River district, which extended on the Great Northern Railway from Big Sandy to Havre, and east all the way to the North Dakota line, and also to the Fort Peck Sioux at Lower Assiniboine Reservation. At this time, the priest apparently lived near the town of Dodson, about twenty miles east of Harlem and just beyond the eastern edge of the Fort Belknap reservation.

Father Eberschweiler compiled a missionary record comparable to that of Protestant missionary "Brother Van," William Wesley Van Orsdel; same God, but different church. The priest was instrumental in erecting churches at Glasgow, Culbertson, Malta, Chinook, Harlem, Great Falls, Lewistown, Oswego, Hinsdale and Havre. At Havre he was appointed first residential priest in 1904 from his former post at Chinook. Again, like "Brother Van," he would buy lots for the churches from his own pocket. The Havre church changed location three times: the first location became the county courthouse and a second combined school/church was built in the present location. Eberschweiler lived long enough to see this and the priest's residence built, but not the present church that was erected in 1924. With three other priests aboard, the work progressed. During the early years the fathers lived in the old Simon Pepin mansion, owned by the Pepin family, with a hall for church services. This thanks to daughter Elizabeth Pepin Meyer.

Now semi-retired, Fr. Eberschweiler had more time to compose songs, write poetry/hymns and complete his literary work, as the other priests tried to do all that he had done by himself.

On October 3, 1908, a special high mass service was held to celebrate Eberschweiler's fifty years as a Jesuit.

The beloved senior priest had not told all his parishioners or area people in advance about his anniversary, so a public non-religious reception was quickly organized for him in the McIntyre Opera House. Colorful green and gold decorations filled the hall along with an orchestra on stage surrounded by potted plants, and three vocalists in attendance. James Holland gave the address of welcome saying that this event gave people the opportunity, "to show their love and regard for this man who had done so much for them and all northern Montana."

Father Eberschweiler in turn reminisced, telling stories of the early days and his life and work among the Indian peoples with all his trials, joys and rewards. The father really didn't want this reception as he was not comfortable with praise or thanks and, as usual, underplayed the hardships he endured to bring some comfort or solace, whether spiritual or physical, to another human creature. He concluded, "thanks to you for your love. May the God of Love grant us all someday an eternal while in heaven."

The Grand Old Man of the Milk River Country died on July 13, 1918 in Havre. A certain Jesuit scholar summed up his value to mankind with the analogy, "the successors of his were products of 'turnips,' but Father Hugo's touch produced 'lilies'."

A fellow Jesuit, David McAstocker, produced a book called, *My Ain Laddie*, edited by a fictitious character called David Dorley. On the surface it is a love story between a lad and his fiancée, Claire. He dropped out of college because of illness, and resides in a mountain home on what is now called Baldy, with a family named McDonnell. He is sick and dying in the Bear's Paw Mountains near Havre and she is back home at "The Oakes" on Long Island. They correspond until she finally comes west when she senses his death is near.

Called Jesuit drama, the work is really aimed at those who had fallen away from the Catholic Church to Protestantism. As a model, McStacker used Eberschweiler, describing him "as a man who refuses to show the toll his many years of missionary work had taken on his body." He wrote that the seventy-year-old priest looked so feeble and haggard that you could scarcely imagine him walking two blocks, but he tramps the prairies like a man scarcely in his forties.

Dorley sees in the old priest's eyes something wistful, something pathetic in his face that moves you to tears, in spite of the generous smile that there must be behind so many battles hidden from the world.

Eberschweiler was indeed that well revered. After his death, his fellow Jesuits said it was impossible to make a reckoning of the good he had accomplished for mankind.

William Wesley Van Orsdel, "Brother Van," 1848-1919

The story of the Methodist Church in Montana is synonymous with the story of the Reverend Mr. Van Orsdel. He is credited with helping to establish 100 churches, 50 parsonages, the Montana Prep School (now Intermountain Children's Home of Montana), Montana Wesleyan University (now Rocky Mountain College), and seven Deaconess hospitals and nurses' quarters.

Like the Jesuit Father Eberschweiler, he was a beloved minister, known for his great faith, vision, enthusiasm and solemn devotion to his purpose of bringing or rekindling religious faith.

The minister eventually became the Methodists' Northern Montana District Superintendent and presiding elder, covering areas that included Augusta, Belt, Hobson, Cascade, Choteau, Fort Benton, Great Falls (home base), Gilt Edge (Lewistown), Harlowton (with Garneill and Judith Gap), Neihart–Monarch, Roundup, Stockett–Sand Coulee, Simms–Sun River, Utica, and their associated organizations.

Van Orsdel's life started on a Pennsylvania farm near Hunterstown, about six miles from Gettysburg. He was the youngest of seven children. His family belonged to the Methodist Episcopal Church, which was formally organized in 1784 as separate from the English Methodist Church.

William Wesley Van Orsdel

He lost both of his parents in his early teens, and he lived with an aunt at Gettysburg while his two older brothers ran the farm. There William continued his practice of attending church regularly and daily praying and reading his Bible. At thirteen he began to run the farm, caring for an aunt and three sisters, when the two older brothers enlisted in the Union Army during the American Civil War. During this period his favorite sister died, gripping his arm, saying, "Will, meet me in Heaven."

When he heard of the great battle to be fought near Gettysburg, he and a friend watched on a hill overlooking the valley. Near the end of their second day of observation, a Confederate military unit under a General Jenkins came upon them. The two convinced the soldiers they were not spies, just local farm boys. Jenkins couldn't elicit any information on the best way to attack the Union forces at Seminary Ridge and moved on. Van Orsdel had witnessed the battle that turned the war in favor of the North. The three-day battle cost the North 3,070 killed and 14,497 wounded; the South lost 2,592 and 12,706 wounded. About 10,000 were missing or captured on both sides. Of course a good number of the wounded died due to infection.

His expertise on the war probably gained audiences when initially his preaching of the Gospel wouldn't. Who of Union loyalty wouldn't want to see and hear of the young boy who had witnessed it, and too, heard Lincoln's battlefield speech and shook the president's hand?

Happily his brothers returned physically unharmed, with Samuel resuming control of the farm operation. Fletcher, Will, and a neighbor formed an evangelistic team and began holding services in local schools and community halls. They continued to hold non-denominational services for six years until 1871, although following Methodist tenets. Their success prompted the nearly 23-year-old to go west to reach people in isolated areas where he felt that he would be even more appreciated.

However, his trip ended two hundred miles later at Oil City, Pennsylvania, with no money, but an immediate job opened up running stationary engines. A rooming house owner allowed him to move in on credit. On Sundays, he acted as a minister in the church-less boomtown. He became so successful that he quit his job after six months. Van Orsdel teamed up with a local boy of a respectable family, and they soon had enough people to form a Methodist congregation. William turned down the pastorship and its generous salary, and continued westward.

Reaching Chicago, Will heard a former Union Army chaplain speak on his incarceration in the Confederacy's notorious Libby prisoner-of-war camp. McCabe reinforced Will's desire to go west, citing the works of the Apostle Paul to build foundations where none exist. The young man returned to Oil City and visited home for a few days before taking the train from Gettysburg on the new lines to Chicago and Sioux City, Iowa. Broke again, he visited the nearest Methodist Church. He stayed temporarily, helping with visitation and services. Again, he turned down an offer to stay and searched for a vessel to take him up the Missouri River to Fort Benton, Montana Territory.

He approached Captain Coulsen, who was supervising the loading of his stern-wheeler, the *Far West*. After some discussion, Coulsen offered Will passage at half price if he would act as chaplain. Will was broke as usual, but was promised that the fifty dollars would be at Pastor Crozier's Methodist Church when Coulsen returned from Montana. Although dubious he was being conned, it was there when he came back.

One day, in South Dakota, Will witnessed a fight between the local Yankton Sioux and an enemy on their hunting lands. Will thought if this is what happens so close to civilization, what will the real West be like? Will also witnessed, in eastern Montana, a band of Lakota Sioux who came aboard in full war regalia when the boat stopped for fuel. The warriors found nothing that interested them, and left with some provisions and trinkets. Sitting Bull and Rain-in-the-Face were supposedly the leaders; they later were leaders of the Sioux Nation against whites' western invasion.

Closer to Fort Benton they saw an unidentified Indian camp with two white women and their children. Brother Van had already received an education about the frontier before he landed.

Will missed the docking at Fort Benton because he was napping. When he awoke, the vessel was deserted, and the crew was celebrating at the Four Deuces Saloon. The date was July 1, 1872, and Will went ashore to find a place for a Sunday service.

He spotted a crowd of people and asked if they knew a place he could hold a Sunday service. The man at the center of the group, District Judge John W. Tattan, offered him the courthouse, but its poor roof was allowing the rain in. Next he tried I.G. Baker's mercantile/trading store. Baker in turn directed him to a Catholic priest, Father Van Garp, who was holding services in a vacant store building owned by T.C. Power, the other merchant prince of the north country. The two got along handsomely, even though in the East, Protestants and Catholics were rarely on friendly terms, nor were the Jesuits with parish priests.

In conversation, Will found that Van Garp had been holding services in Montana, and was on his way back to St. Louis. Both discovered they had suffered the horrors of war, yet Will was only now having his first bout with boot-sucking, wet gumbo mud! Brother Van stayed for the priest's last service, enjoying his sermon on "What does it profit a man if he gained the whole world, [but] he lost his soul?" Van Garp introduced Van Orsdel after the service, who announced he would hold both a 3:00 P.M. and an 8:00 P.M. service. He escorted the priest to his boat, then returned to the *Far West* for a nap.

Some people become a legend in their own time, like Davey Crockett when shot a "bare" at age three. In Brother Van's case, his legend began when he held services in a saloon, and he wowed the crowd made up of gamblers, gunmen and prostitutes.

He did in fact have a cross-section of humanity—cowboys, soldiers, steamboat crewmen, businessmen, ranchers, and more. He began by introducing himself, then breaking into song with old standards such as "The Old Rugged Cross." Between songs he quoted scripture and offered prayers. His fears of the Wild West started to disappear when the crowd responded warmly. After the service he became "Brother Van" since the worshipers said William Wesley Van Orsdel was too long to handle.

Mrs. George Baker, sister-in-law of I.G. Baker, invited Van

Orsdel to stay at the family home while in Fort Benton. She attended both his services, adding to the civility of the day. She and husband George Baker became the minister's life-long friends.

Brother Van next hitched a rain-soaked ride with a teamster to the town and river crossing of Sun River. There was located the northernmost military post in Montana, called Fort Shaw. Upon arrival he secured a place to stay with the Charles Bull family and used their home for services. After a large festive meal for worshipers, Brother Van went to nearby Fort Shaw and held a service, returning to Sun River for an evening service. With some of his friends giving guidance, he went to the Blackfeet (Piegan) Indian Agency near the town of Choteau. The loan of a large white horse, named Jonathan, became a gift and allowed him to move on to Helena. He found the home of the minister and presiding elder of the Helena district of the Methodist Church, J.A. Van Anda. Van Anda explained that Montana Territory included only the one parsonage church in Helena, with only ninety-five known Methodists and five Sunday schools. Brother Van led the evening service, singing many songs, including his favorite, which was a sermon in itself, called "Diamonds in the Rough."

The senior elder thought that Van Orsdel should be a Methodist missionary at large under his general supervision. The following year the young man would be eligible for a regular appointment at the Rocky Mountain conference in Salt Lake City. So, off he went without salary, "to spread scriptural holiness throughout the land."

For the next ten years he did exactly that, stopping at farms, ranches and towns trying—and succeeding—in fostering an interest in establishing Sunday schools and then churches.

The places he stopped at became homes on the road where food and shelter were always available to him. He had many, many good experiences, but once in a while life took a strange turn, as when a rancher dropped him off at Radersburg on his way to Bozeman. He found the streets nearly deserted, with people scurrying indoor and peeking through windows until a band of armed citizens approached him. He used his only defense by standing on a wagon and singing. He learned from the people that they thought he was a gunman/horse thief reported in the area. Will believed if he ran he would have been shot.

Brother Van became an official junior preacher in the summer of 1873, and served under the Baltimore-educated scholar Reverend Francis Asbury Riggin in the gold-rush towns of Bannack and Virginia City. The two 25-year-olds made a great pair: Riggin with great sermons, Brother Van with his music and ability to bring many forward to repent. They held many revival services, even reaching into northern Idaho.

The two became so successful that their circuit was split up, with Brother Van keeping Bannack and adding Sheridan to its northeast. Two years later, this assignment put him almost in the path of the Nez Perce Indians' trek from Idaho, as they attempted to reach their Crow (Absarokee) allies in southeast Montana. Fleeing the army, the Nez Perce approached Brother Van's circuit, particularly after the Battle of the Big Hole when they appeared to be heading to Bannack. Van Orsdel arrived to find the town's citizens organized into a militia, with dirt-and-log barricades erected around Bannack. Women and children were placed in the local hotel. Brother Van held a service that night where the "fox hole spirituality" sent the bulk of residents not on guard duty.

No attack came, but two men did struggle in, reporting killings by Nez Perce in the Horse Prairie country to the southwest. Brother Van accompanied the rescue party to a ranch where four bodies were found. They managed to escape with a body when the Nez Perce fired on them, and then found the rancher alive as well. Back at Bannack, Will and John Poindexter volunteered to find the military units tracking the Nez Perce. They did and brought a company of cavalry back to town. Then they volunteered to carry a message to the Bannack–Virginia City stagecoach. He finished off his work by having the cooped-up citizens and military build a church.

Brother Van moved on to the Bitterroot River Valley, along the north-side valley where the Bitterroot entered the Clark Fork River near Missoula. His path took him to the Big Hole battlefield, where a severe thunderstorm forced him to camp for two days. The rain torrent washed up bodies of both soldiers and Nez Perce alike. Upon reaching civilization he sent word to Fort Missoula of the battlefield burial situation. His involvement in the aftermath continued when he conducted funerals for the volunteers who had fought under Colonel John Gibbons' force from Fort Shaw.

Southwest of the Bitterroot country was Beaverhead County, with its seat at Dillon, the terminus of the Utah and Northern Railway. There a Sister Selway conducted Methodist services at the Poindexter School. Brother Van conducted a service there, and he stayed overnight with the Reynolds family, where he became infatuated with the thirteen-year-old daughter, Jeanie. Over the years, their relationship grew until they were engaged. However, her family felt she first needed to complete two years of college. But, during her first year at Northwestern University, she became ill and died on October 20, 1881, at the age of eighteen. Before the burial Van Orsdel placed a wedding ring on her finger.

He continued with his work philosophy of "a church in every community and a yearly renewal in every church." Wherever he preached he left a core of people who kept the faith by continuing the Sunday school. As their numbers grew, he successfully solicited funds for a church and parsonage.

The stories of his faith and courage are legion, even to the tale of his employing sympathetic gunmen to stop unruly ones from breaking up revival meetings at Missoula.

Brother Van rejoined his old preaching partner, Francis Asbury Riggin, on the Fort Benton–Great Falls circuit in 1887. From their base at Fort Benton, the newly created town of Great Falls became the next objective.

A serious illness slowed him down temporarily, and then he recuperated at the residence of Riggin and his wife. Brother Van continued in various positions of the church, leaving as Great Falls District Superintendent in 1913 and becoming Superintendent of the Milk River–Glasgow district. However, his only home was a room in the new parsonage.

Two memorable events happened in northern Montana. First, early in his career, he went on a buffalo hunt with Piegan Blackfeet, bringing down a buffalo with his eyes closed. And, second, conducting a service in Landusky at an abandoned saloon where Harvey "Kid Curry" Logan had killed Powell "Pike" Landusky.

If he had one indulgence, it was his yearly birthday party in Fort Benton. For Van Orsdel's seventieth-birthday party in 1918, Charlie Russell was among hordes of admirers, but couldn't come because of jury duty. He instead sent a letter with an original sketch of a steamboat on the Missouri River with a large herd of buffalo stopping its progress. "Kid" Russell had been a fan of Brother Van since they first met in Judith Basin country of central Montana.

Father Eberschweiler also had a soft spot for Fort Benton, having been the first resident priest there. Eberschweiler had died a year earlier in Havre, and Van Orsdel would soon follow.

One of his favorite families were the Reigels, who had a sawmill at Landusky. Mr. Reigel became the local Sunday superintendent. Their daughter, Leafy, became his secretary. Usually whatever home or town was his temporary home base, a resident became his secretary, too. In October of 1919, he was staying with the Reigels—now Chinook residents—working with Leafy and catching up with his paperwork. When they started to leave for a reception at the local school for the new pastor and wife, he couldn't get his arm into his coat sleeve. He fell unconscious a few seconds later. They moved him to his upstairs bedroom and the doctor was called. The doctor explained that he had suffered a stroke with paralysis on his left side, although his brain seemed unaffected. He rallied enough to receive visitors before being moved to the Deaconess Hospital in Great Falls, which had been one of his many projects.

As December began, Brother Van made his final plans for a funeral and its committee, and completed his annual Christmas cards as well as he could, before dying ten minutes after midnight on December 19. He opened his eyes just before death, barely lifted his right hand and pronounced he was going home. After the funeral, he was buried in Helena at the Forestvale Cemetery, near the Deaconess School he had founded. As a final tribute, the children and staff of the school placed a small tree with their handmade decorations, and sang Christmas carols.

Brother Van had considerable property when he died, in fact he planned to retire to a Flathead Lake property he owned. Some of the property was given to brother Fletcher, the rest given to the Deaconess School, Montana Wesleyan University in Billings, and the Great Falls Deaconess Hospital.

Since Brother Van's only real home was at the First Methodist Church's parsonage in Great Falls, a Brother Van Experience Committee in 2000 was formed at the church, now First United Methodist Church, first placing the parsonage on the National Register of Historic Places and then beginning to raise money to have the home restored.

Both Eberschweiler and Van Orsdel, though of different Christian faiths, gave the same message of live the faith, pray without ceasing, read the Bible with God-centered faith.

They both exhibited love for all, and never ceased laboring until their dying breaths.

Modest living, God-fearing, they were grand old men of the Milk River Valley whose very presence was a blessing to all people.

Master of Many Trades
Louis Shambo, 1846-1918

Louis "Louie" Shambo stood above most of the rugged, tough individuals of the Milk River country, with the exciting and interesting life he had experienced among the Métis (mixed blood) buffalo hunters, as an Indian fighter and Indian friend, and U.S. Army scout, horse or mule supply packer, wagon freighter, cowboy, bartender and rancher.

Reportedly Shambo talked little about his life, even turning down a Texas book publisher who wanted to publish his biography, saying he didn't need money or want the publicity. Only close friends heard his stories, and when someone outside his circle began probing for information, he changed the subject.

Hence it took a lot of work and patience to put his biography together. He opened up to Chinook author A.J. Noyes only in 1916 about his purported involvement in the last battle (in 1877) of the Nez Perce on their flight from Idaho. Here is what his friends and acquaintances—especially Vina Sterling—were able to piece together.

Louie Shambo was of French descent, although some

Louis Shambo

said he might have had some Cree or Chippewa heritage too. It was believed he was born in New Orleans, Louisiana about 1846, while other accounts place his birth in St. Paul, Minnesota, which would account for those who thought he had a Métis heritage (French-Chippewa or French-Cree). The most reliable account has his family moving to St. Paul in about 1852, to be near some relatives. His father's occupation is not known, but farming or ranching would be a good guess.

When Louie later worked for the U.S. Army, his original surname of "Chambeau" became "Shambo" and sometimes "Shambeau."

Shambo attended a Roman Catholic school that was located in St. Paul. Because of the long walk to town, his father bought an Indian pony for Louis and his sister Mary to ride, making the school trip enjoyable. The young man soon encountered the Chippewa Indian people of the area, befriending them and learning their language and customs (Shambo turned out to be an amateur ethnologist, but never had the education to write up his experiences). What interested Shambo the most, though, were the tales of the Wild West. He permanently left his family behind when he joined an Indian or Métis group at the ripe old age of twelve in 1858, heading west on his blue-gray pony with a rope bridle, without benefit of a saddle.

His first journey took him only a few miles to the settlement of Pembina, Dakota Territory, on the Red River. Here Shambo was really exposed to a colorful Métis colony with French and English traders, Cree and other Chippewa peoples. Several trading companies had been established there, because of the commerce trail then running between Fort Garry (future Winnipeg, Manitoba) and St. Paul. The Métis, he would have learned, hauled their goods in high-wheeled Red River carts, each drawn by a pony or ox, and made entirely of wood except for the wheel rims that were covered with shrunken rawhide. One cart could carry a load of 500 to 900 pounds depending on the animal. The noise of the wood hubs rubbing against the axle could be heard for miles.

Joseph Kinsey Howard described the sound as "a tooth-stabbing screech which was never forgotten by anyone who heard it; it was as if a thousand finger nails were drawn across a thousand panes of glass."

Shambo would have traveled in a brigade of ten carts with a walking teamster for every three or so. In fact, most of the men walked the same thousand miles per hunting season. Howard said the brigades "would cross the prairie like a great snake, the extra horses or oxen fanning out beside the carts." At their peak, there was as many as 2500 carts on the buffalo trails, organized as well as any army.

And, along with the unusual transportation, were their colorful dress with bright-beaded designs in buckskin or wool, and the male with his hand-sewed "Assumption" (Quebec) sash, tied around the waist or looped over a shoulder. His headgear consisted of a handmade wool pillbox, braided in beads or porcupine quills. The women wore silk heads carves along with embroidered shawls or aprons. Both sexes wore moccasins that constantly wore out. Shambo wouldn't have stuck out in his costume, because many Métis were more blue-eyed-blond-French than Indian in appearance.

According to his accounts, Shambo spent about seven years in the Dakota Territory and present-day Saskatchewan hunting buffalo before coming to the Milk River Country, near the end of the American Civil War. Since few there spoke English, he came in handy as an interpreter; he claimed to know six Indian languages, along with French and English.

When the buffalo were in the millions and spread over several territories, no treaty Indian people overly worried about the Métis' mass hunting, vacuum-cleaner techniques until the buffalo was nearly exterminated. The "Slotas" as the Lakota Sioux called them, were tolerated because they provided them with the latest weaponry, ammunition and other trade goods, especially whiskey. Juneaux's Post on Frenchman's Creek twelve miles upstream from its mouth, was a major trading post of the Métis. Only when

Métis hunters intruded deep into Sioux hunting grounds did they clash—and Shambo was involved in several of these fights.

Historian Robert M. Utley wrote of some of these violent clashes between Sitting Bull's forces and the Métis, first in 1873 when a trading session near Fort Peck at the confluence of Big Dry with the Missouri River turned violent because too much whiskey was distributed. A few months later, the same Lakota Sioux fought a group of two or three hundred Métis, who had crossed the Yellowstone River and moved south on the Rosebud River in the heart of Sioux country. Sitting Bull sent a hundred warriors to attack their camp, but the Métis had gone into a defensive position with corralled wagons and earthen breastworks. They opened fire with lever-action rifles and a cannon. The Sioux wisely retreated before they were completely wiped out.

Whether Shambo was in these actions is unknown, but he did speak of some battles. One such occurred on the Jim (James) River at Strawberry Lake. No tribe was mentioned, but since the river is located in the Dakotas, presumably it was Lakota or Yanktonai Sioux. The Métis caravan was stopped at the lake by the Sioux, who told them to go back, but the Métis leader replied that they were going to follow the buffalo. The ensuing battle probably included corralled wagons, and lasted three days, according to Shambo, until "…we licked the hell out of them and made them run." The Indian forces retreated to the Sheyenne River, which parallels the James River to the east in present-day southeastern North Dakota.

Shambo also spoke of a battle on the White Earth River; it entered the Missouri River east of present-day Williston, North Dakota. This would have been traditional Assiniboine Indian lands. The Assiniboine were an offshoot of the Yanktonai Nakota Sioux. Shambo claimed that they killed forty Sioux, and the Métis only lost six or seven fighters.

The one battle he talked about in detail occurred on the "Pochette." There is such a creek that flows into the Missouri, south of present-day Malta and northwest of the Little Rocky Mountains.

However, there is also Frenchman's Creek that flows south from Canada, and enters the Milk River west of Malta. At the time, there were only four men in a Métis hunting party when they encountered perhaps twenty-five Indian warriors. These could have been from any of several Canada or U.S. Indian peoples who hunted on the plains. In a two-hour battle, Shambo was shot in the shoulder, and another Métis killed; in return they killed five or six of the attacking party. Shambo laughingly told author Noyes that, "...no gentleman would try to interfere with a person when he was trying to make a living, don't you think so?"

In about 1877, at thirty-seven or so, he decided to leave the Métis people, probably camped on the Milk River, and he headed south to the Bighorn River country of Montana, taking two friends and living with the Crow Indian people for a two-year visit. His mixed-blood friend became lonely and rejoined his people while Shambo's other unnamed friend went with him into the Wyoming and Colorado country, spending perhaps the next three years with both the Cheyenne and Shoshone Indian peoples.

Next the restless pair went west to Nevada, where they worked for a large cattle ranch for two years. They tried California, but found it not to their liking, and returned to employment with the Nevada ranch. They then got a chance to return to Montana in about 1883 with a cattle herd bought by Howell and Jack Harris, for a ranch located south of Fort Benton, the innermost Missouri River steamboat port. The Harrises were employed by the Benton and St. Louis Circle Cattle Company, the largest ranch in Montana at the time.

Shambo and his friend helped bring the herd north, but returned to Nevada for another year. This seems to clash with Shambo's dates of being employed by the army, however, unless he did both simultaneously. Shambo's friend died before the next trip to Montana the following year. The second cattle herd were sold to the Broadwater-McColloh Company at the military Fort Assinniboine, where the two partners had the post trader's contract. Simon Pepin and L.K. Devlin ran the beef operation. They had heard of the high-quality Nevada beef from Howell Harris. Pepin sent cowboys Charles Harvey, Tom McDevitt and John Kinsella to accompany the beef back to Montana. They would become lifelong friends of Shambo's.

This time Shambo stayed in Montana, working for the Charles Broadwater enterprise in several capacities, such as teamster, butcher, and cowboy. He helped haul logs from the Sucker Creek wood camp in the Bear's Paw Mountains, and hauled supplies to the fall military mountain camps near Mount Otis when the troops were on maneuvers. In between he worked for the military as needed, including carrying dispatches back and forth to Fort Walsh in the Cypress Hills of present-day Saskatchewan. He and another man carried the post payroll in money belts, supposedly from Denver, Colorado. But perhaps the earlier payrolls came up the Missouri River to Fort Benton or from Helena where the state military headquarters was now located.

Shambo said that on their rides they saw hangings, presumably by vigilantes, but they kept their distance and never inquired. On one trip, Shambo asserted they were being followed by two tough-looking characters. Stopping for the night, they told the rancher about their pursuers. After supper the rancher and his hired man disappeared on a ride. On their return they told Shambo to relax and get some sleep, as they wouldn't be bothered anymore again; no questions were asked.

One of his more exciting scouting operations occurred in the 1880s with some Plains Cree Indians at Wild Horse Lake, north of the fort between the Milk River and the international border. The military scouts first found the hostiles with stolen horses, and engaged them in a firefight before the main military body arrived. Some Cree were captured and others killed; also some of the stolen horses were killed or wounded. Shambo would have been accompanied by Gros Ventre scouts, who by treaty lived in north-central Montana. The army clashed many times with Canadian Indians, especially the Plains Cree.

Shambo married a Gros Ventre woman, and they had perhaps

four children. The army allowed civilian employees to live in cabins north of the fort on Beaver Creek.

Shambo moved to the newly established railroad town of Havre in 1891, renting a small house from Tom McDevitt. By that point it is believed his lonely wife and children had moved back to Fort Belknap and lived with her family. Shambo spent the summers working for the P-Cross ranches of Simon Pepin, along with other friends, including foreman Charles Harvey. Shambo was the ranch's top horse wrangler, and did the same work for lawman George Bickle at his ranch south of town. Shambo had worked at Bickle's saloon in the army tent town of Cypress on Big Sandy Creek. It had consisted of several saloons and brothels, plus a hardware store. Shambo worked at Bailey & Purnell's saloon once he lived in Havre; it was owned by two former military men. He lived on a homestead in 1917 on the former fort reservation near a creek now bearing his name. He followed his favorite pastime of raising horses. There also, at a later date, was a Shambo School, a mail route and a veterinary clinic in Havre.

Friend and neighbor Vina Harvey described him as a man who "...lived a clean life, dressed well and was a modest gentleman." He spent many hours at Bailey & Purnell's saloon in retirement, visiting with old friends, and also at Bruce Clyde's livery barn. Charles Harvey had died and Vina married Bruce. Vina said that, in passing friends, Shambo only said hello once in a day, and he was puzzled why others said it more than once in a day to the same people!

In 1917 his heart condition worsened, and he sold off some of his horses to the government. His family operated the ranch until it was proofed up, then sold it to the Clydes. During this time a brother whom Shambo had never met came to Havre. He was in town doing business for the Great Northern Railway. Shambo hadn't seen his family since leaving St. Paul; they must have had a lot to catch up on.

Shambo died at the Sacred Heart Hospital in November of 1918, renewing his Catholicism before his death.

This should have been the end of his story—except in his last few years he opened up to Chinook author A.J. Noyes about his participation as a scout in the Great Sioux War of 1876-1877, and the last stand of the non-treaty Nez Perce at Snake Creek in the Bear's Paw Mountains. Noyes came to Havre in about 1910 from the Big Hole Valley, at Wisdom, where he ranched and operated a gold mine. He was a member of the volunteer army raised at Butte by "Major" William A. Clark to fight the retreating Nez Perce. However, the Nez Perce took a more southerly route through the Bitterroot River Valley and traveled into the Big Hole in their quest to link up with the Crow Indians. Noyes was quite happy to include Shambo's account since few details were available at that time. It would be a few years before autobiographies from army commanders would be written. Unfortunately, Shambo's story is not verifiable, and has many inconsistencies.

At the beginning of the Nez Perce chapter, Noyes tells the general story of the Nez Perce people, their flight and battles across Idaho and Montana, concluding with the Snake Creek battle, south of present-day Chinook. Next comes his introduction of Shambo with "the scout who found the Nez Perce camp for [Colonel] Miles was Louis Shambrow [sic] at this time [December 1916] living in Havre. I'm going to allow him to give his description as I consider it very interesting and because it had never been given to the public."

Shambo told Noyes of being with General George Crook's army that was based at Fort Kearney and Fort Russell in Wyoming Territory. Crook wasn't part of either the Montana or Yellowstone military district, but headquartered at Fort Omaha, Nebraska. Shambo, though, claimed he accompanied Miles' top scout Luther "Yellowstone" Kelly and Crook's troops to the eastern Montana tributaries of the Missouri River before meeting up with Colonel Nelson Miles at his Fort Keogh headquarters near Miles City. He said initially Miles wouldn't offer enough money to be his scout, but finally agreed on $125.00 per month.

He began his job by accompanying Miles' troops into the Little Missouri River country. That stream flows through the southeast corner of Montana, from Wyoming, up to North Dakota and then joins the Missouri River. Miles called the unit back to join in cutting off the Nez Perce from reaching Canada. The pursuing troops of General Howard and Colonel Sturgis were far behind. The Indians had crossed the Missouri at Cow Creek, looting a wagon train and burning what they couldn't carry. Miles told Shambo to go back to Fort Keogh and break in some mules, instead of accompanying the troops. Shambo's stay at Keogh was short, however, as he had to bring messages to Miles' command, and was allowed to stay since he knew the Bear's Paw Mountains–Milk River Country so well.

Miles' chief scout was Luther S. "Yellowstone" Kelly. Shambo is not mentioned in either of Miles' or Kelly's autobiographies, but others were. Miles spoke of Kelly as best of the best, only equaled by such national heroes as Daniel Boone and Davey Crockett. General Miles was also proud of the fact that Kelly later became an army officer.

Kelly was directed to find the Nez Perce's trail, and camp with his fellow soldier-scouts, which they did. Soldier-scout Milan Tripp reported back to Colonel Miles that they had found the Nez Perce trail through the mountains. Miles arrived with his Sioux and Cheyenne scouts of the 7th and 2nd Cavalry and 5th Infantry. The attack began at dawn.

Noyes, on the other hand, claimed Shambo, accompanied by ten Cheyenne scouts belonging to Miles, found the trail and the Nez Perce camp on Snake Creek.

Shambo set the scene with the first charge of soldiers, himself in the lead, of deaths of men and horses, and how the Nez Perce sharpshooters had them pinned down after the charges failed. He said his horse was killed, and he was using it for cover until it was shot to pieces and smelled horrible. He then scrambled behind a rock, huddling with fellow scouts Kelly and Corporal John Haddo. Haddo was seriously wounded; Kelly and Shambo attempted to carry him back of the lines, to the wagons, but he died on the way. Kelly returned later, bringing him a horse.

Kelly, in his later autobiography, wrote that he had been behind a ridge with Haddo trying to spot the Indian snipers. Haddo was using Kelly's field glasses and stood up receiving a bullet in the chest. By that time, Kelly was back with the wagons eating a meal. Only upon his return had he discovered Haddo's death.

Shambo's criticism of Miles' tactics, his account of Nez Perce sharpshooters' accuracy, his dramatic story of using the dead horse for cover, the rock where he was pinned down, and Haddo's killing made it into Merrill D. Beal's 1963 book *I Will Fight No More Forever: Chief Joseph and the Nez Perce*, which used only Noyes' book as a source.

Shambo's friends accounted for the two conflicting stories of his life in 1876-1877, by saying he left Fort Assinniboine, going with Crook and Miles in the Great Sioux War and Nez Perce conflict, and then returning to the fort in 1877. However, Fort Assinniboine wasn't built until 1879. Until then, Fort Keogh and Buford were the two forts dealing with the eastern Montana Indian peoples. While the details of Shambo's life are in conflict, he still remains a hero of the Milk River Country.

Ranch Woman Extraordinaire

Ellen Thompson, 1851–1895

THE CHINOOK OPINION of May 2, 1895, had its usual town, country and state news items, including deaths, accidents and business happenings. There were no births that day. Captain F.L. Tracy had dropped dead at a Great Falls saloon. The Great Northern Railway was changing the route of its tracks between Big Sandy, Verona and Great Falls. Also a local couple lost their baby daughter in spite of the doctor's best efforts, and a Harlem, Montana, woman was struck by a passenger train at Saco, Montana, about 100 miles to the east.

The main topic, though, was the death of Mrs. William Thompson Sr. The obituary stated she had been "a fearful sufferer for the last years," and she had recently returned from the Great Falls hospital. She apparently was a victim of cancer and didn't survive her surgery. The article went on to say that she was forty-four years of age, was born in Manchester, England and had

William and Ellen Thompson. BONNIE WILLIAMSON, HAVRE

been a Montana resident for about ten years, seven of those years locally, living along Peoples Creek.

The funeral at the Method-ist-Episcopal Church was a

large one, with an "impressive and very effecting [sic] funeral sermon was preached by Reverend Allan Rodges [Rogers]..." Afterwards, "the funeral procession was a very long one and was composed of all the best people of the town and vicinity. Mrs. Thompson leaves a husband [William] and a large family to mourn her loss."

Perhaps the first white woman settler to live in the Milk River Country in what is now Blaine County, deserves more of her story told, beyond that of being a faithful wife and mother. (As for "first white woman," it is true that an Indian agent, W.L. Lincoln, at the Fort Belknap trading post/Indian agency had brought his wife and daughter along in about 1878, but they were not settlers.)

From the sketchy biographical details available, we see that both William and Ellen (Dalton) Thompson came to North America from Great Britain: he from somewhere in Wales, and she from England; they met and married in Manchester. Presumably the Dalton family lived well since they owned a dye-fabric factory in London.

They migrated to Philadelphia at an unknown date. With them came their three boys: William, Gerald and Frank. William's occupation at that time is unknown, although his later jobs showed a proficiency in handling and taming horses. Two more boys were born in that city, Robert and Charles (the latter possibly in Winnipeg, then Canada's jumping-off town for its western frontier), before they moved to the Dominion of Canada to escape the American Civil War in 1860.

The Thompsons first moved to Fort Qu'Appelle in present-day Saskatchewan. There, the westbound Canadian Pacific Railroad tracks abruptly ended, with only the rugged frontier beyond. The town and trading post were "the focal point of a network of prairie trails by which the first wave of settlers entered the west." The Qu'Appelle River Valley and adjacent glacial lakes was a major trading center for the British Hudson's Bay Company.

The fort became a major staging area for the North West Mounted Police and Canadian Militia in the 1885 Northwest Rebellion or Resistance by the Métis (French-Indian) people under Louis Reil, over land rights.

The Thompsons decided to leave the Qu'Appelle area when the conflict broke out in 1885, although the war was soon over and never touched them. They loaded their covered wagon and journeyed the three hundred some miles via the major trail southwest to Fort Walsh, and then south past Fort Assinniboine to Fort Benton, Montana Territory. With them came three additional family members: Margaret, Mary and Emma.

At Fort Benton, William secured employment as a teamster for one of the city's major merchant companies, probably I.G. Baker & Brother. That business had begun in the U.S. buffalo robe and fur trade, then branched into Canada as a major supplier and transporter of goods for the government, Indian reserves, and its own trading stores. Baker and other such companies also held contracts with the U.S. Army. Thompson probably learned of Fort Benton because the I.G. Baker Company's supply wagons traveled to Fort Qu'Appelle.

In the latter months of summer-into-fall, the heavy-laden steamboats couldn't reach Fort Benton because of seasonally low water in the Missouri River, and the boats' cargoes had to be dropped off at such downstream landings as Cow Island, Rocky Point, Wolf Point, and even Devil's Lake, Dakota Territory, where the Great Northern Railway's western progress had stopped.

In addition, Thompson would have learned from the traders that the railroad was to move westward soon, through the Milk River Country, once permission came to lay track, for a fee, through Indian reservations. He believed that the opening of settlement lands would soon follow the railroad's path.

After a year or so in Fort Benton, Thompson moved his family, circa 1886, to the western beginning of Peoples Creek, a southern tributary of the Milk River. His claim was near an outcropping of rock on the south side of the Bear's Paw Mountains. He placed his family in a small log cabin set in a meadow near where a small stream flowed.

Thompson may have found this ideal place by venturing or freighting north from the Cow Island Trail, following along the east side of the Bear's Paws to the Fort Belknap trading post. The Métis/Indian/military trail or trails went quite near, or crossing, Peoples Creek. This "Pierre's Trail" also intersected with a trail to nearby Fort Assinniboine.

Peoples Creek starts in the mountains, flowing eastward across the prairies through the present-day Fort Belknap Indian Reservation. For the first two years the family was on its own with their only white neighbors located at either Fort Belknap to the north or Fort Assinniboine to the northwest. The land belonged principally to the Gros Ventre Indian tribe. When the northern lands were designated as belonging to the Blackfoot Confederacy in the treaties of 1851 and 1855, the Gros Ventre (Arapaho) were conveniently lumped in as residents. Also lumped into the eastern part of northern Montana were the River Crow and several bands of the Upper Missouri River Assiniboine.

Apparently the Thompsons had a spacious piece of land that later allowed them, under subsequent land acts, to own up to 800 acres.

The day Ellen saw her husband ride out of sight on his way back to Fort Benton must have been one of her worst, and she would hardly have been thinking about what a pleasing location they had. Here she was, out in the middle of nowhere with all her children. The nearest assistance was at either Fort Assinniboine or Fort Belknap. It would have to be a very serious situation to seek help since they were then on the land illegally, subject to eviction.

It would be about two years before she would see any fellow settlers. If she exchanged mail with her distant family it only came with her husband's infrequent visits. Ellen had not lived in "civilization" for several years by then. Fort Qu'Appelle in the Canadian wilderness hadn't been; Fort Benton was somewhat better. Did she have friends as well as relatives that she missed?

And too, she faced this daunting task with only one good arm. She had lost the use of her other at Fort Qu'Appelle when she severely burned it up to the shoulder. At the time she was struggling with a can of coal oil to light a fire in the wood-stove, with baby William in her arms. The can's contents caught fire and exploded. Ellen shielded the baby with her arm as her clothing caught fire. After it healed, the arm functioned only to push things around, with apparently little hand function. The children would rap on the shriveled arm to hear its "hollow" sound.

But she had no time to feel sorry for herself. She must cope. So this "little bit of woman" plunged into organizing her family for survival. The older boys would have to carry heavy burdens of responsibilities.

The family's first winter would have been the most challenging. Mother Nature brought the worst winter that the white settlers of Montana, Wyoming, Colorado, western Nebraska and Kansas had ever seen.

During the previous summer, the lands south of the Missouri River contained an overabundance of cattle, and grass had become scarce due to severe drought along with overgrazing. Winter brought heavy snow, driving winds, and extreme cold. At the military post of Fort Keogh, in eastern Montana, the temperature registered sixty degrees below zero on January 14, 1887, with two feet of snow on the ground. By March 15, the range was littered with thousands of rotten cattle carcasses.

The weather is recorded, the Thompson family's life in that cabin is not. Ellen was certainly at a disadvantage with a one-room residence and nine children. Some of the "richer" families at least had a separate adult bedroom and loft for the children to sleep in. The combination kitchen, living room, bathing and laundry room must have been claustrophobic. Ellen apparently didn't have a washer boiler, and had to heat water on the stove for cooking or bathing. What furniture she possessed was probably handmade, with boxes and pegs nailed to the walls for storage. Usually the bed frames and rails consisted of wood poles and smaller pieces of wood to support the mattresses, which were stuffed with hay covered in cloth remnants (ticking). Her china from England seemed to be her most precious belonging, used only on special occasions instead of the tinware.

If sick, they had to rely on home remedies such as steam from the kettle, goat grease on the body, mustard plasters, alcohol, cold compresses or a rubbing alcohol-sulfur-lard mix on skin, daily castor oil, and disinfecting carbolic acid.

And, what of the outside? Did the family plant a garden in the spring? Were berries picked, oats and alfalfa raised, and a barn built for animals? Did the livestock include a milk cow, chickens and a horse to pull the single-axle wagon? Was a root cellar dug to keep the vegetables, meat, milk, etc.? We hope so.

Meanwhile Ellen would have had to set up some kind of routine, such as cleaning clothes, bodies and the outhouse on Saturdays. The girls had to learn to heat the flat iron on the coolest part of the stove so as not to scorch the clothes. Mending clothes was another never-ending chore. Milking the cow resulted in the chores of separating out the cream and using some of the skim milk to make cottage cheese, and the rest for cooking. The cream aided in cooking, along with being used in the breakfast oats. A treat was homemade bread with cream, cinnamon and sugar. Butter was churned from the cream, then stored in a root cellar under cloth. Berries would yield jams, jellies and syrups. A priority was the quick processing of fresh meat through cooking, smoking, etc. The boys probably hunted between storms, besides shoveling paths through the snow to the barn and outhouse.

The list of duties went on and on.

William's first trip home in the spring brought much needed supplies and emotional relief, perhaps even mail or a present of cloth, candy, or the like.

Warmer spring weather allowed wet laundry to be put outside to dry instead of being draped over every piece of furniture. Homemade lye soap served for both washing and bathing.

During the second year of their residence, the land opened for legal settlement, bringing much-needed companionship and neighbors for mutual assistance.

The now open reservation lands brought in the last of the large cattle ranchers with many thousands of both Texas longhorns and Oregon shorthorns. The creeks to the north became favorite pasture land with their mountain water, where brush and taller trees gave both summer shade and winter shelter. The large Bear Paw Cattle Pool was headquartered at foreman L.B. Taylor's ranch on Bean Creek near the new community of Lloyd. Soon the settlement had a general store and post office. The Thompsons now had access to supplies and a piece of the outside world.

The Fort Belknap trading post closed and its store moved to the new community of Chinook on the Great Northern Railway. The Indian agency moved east to its new location near the town called Harlem.

The cattle ranchers also provided a relief for the Thompsons, both in housing and in income, because the older boys could be farmed out to work. Besides, they needed the space: Ellen was pregnant again, and gave birth to her last child, John, on November 17, 1890. William had returned permanently, and had a ready market in providing gentled horses to ranchers and townspeople. Thus Ellen surely had had an escort to take her to the Bert Cain ranch where a Mrs. Gray was the midwife. Now a white child had been born in the country.

The nearby Gros Ventre and Assiniboine people marveled at the "paleface papoose." They would come and sit by his cradle for hours at a time. Ellen had no fear, and she was kind to them, sharing food; and in turn, they gave baby John beaded vests, fur caps and moccasins. Some even offered to trade ponies for him. The younger children were not so brave, and hid under the beds when their families dropped by.

Sometime in that period, many Indian people died. Since the buffalo were now gone, the Indians' living conditions were pitiful, and disease and starvation prevailed. The Thompsons saw many burials in a grove of trees, wrapped in blankets and bound to branches with buckskin strips.

The following summer, Ellen and the younger children received an invitation to a small Fourth of July picnic at the Grays' house on the George Mundt ranch near Lloyd. Ellen walked, somehow carrying John and an umbrella, and holding Emma by the hand. The two older girls, Maggie and Mamie, rode double on the horse. The family came upon a herd of skittish longhorn cattle that blocked their path. The herd stampeded at their approach and in their direction. With nowhere to run, the children and horse moved instinctively behind Ellen.

Ellen must have handed John to a daughter because she opened and closed her umbrella towards the menacing cattle, causing the herd to divide and run around them. They finally made it to the picnic, only Mamie fell off the horse, broke her nose and ruined her dress. Ellen even put a clothes pin on the bleeding nose once they reached their destination.

Although Ellen visited neighbors around Lloyd, she apparently never ventured to the local trading center of Chinook. At the least, most settlers of that country visited the town every six months for supplies. Her second oldest son, Gerald or "Jerry," operated a livery stable there. However she had to have visited somewhere—perhaps Fort Benton—when she filed for citizenship in 1888.

The Thompson family had to move to Chinook in 1895 due to Ellen's having a severe illness, probably cancer. She had suffered for two years before undergoing surgery in Great Falls. She died shortly after returning to Chinook. The remaining Thompsons stayed in Chinook for a period of time before going on an ill-fated adventure to Bottineau, North Dakota, then to somewhere in Alabama, and returned to the Chinook area after about three years.

William acquired a new piece of land, since he had sold the original property before leaving Chinook. It was not the choice piece of property he originally owned. He made a meager living by buying sheep on shares and raising them. Thompson died in 1900, perhaps from diabetes. He had been in Great Falls for four months, although it wasn't specified whether that residence was medically related.

The youngest child, John, nearly 11, now lived with brother

Bob and his wife, Agnes. Their home was east of the old Thompson place near the community of Maddux, in an area called "Hungary Hollow." In 1901, settlers there had suffered from a lack of food through the winter because the thin-layered soil produced such poor crops. Bob Thompson was one of the few who survived. John attended school and Sunday school at Maddux, which also had a community church. John became a major cattle rancher in the area, and he was said to have "built up one of the best Hereford cattle herds," becoming well known at the Chicago and St. Paul cattle markets.

Apparently the two youngest daughters lived with their oldest sister, Margaret; she lived in the Lloyd area with her rancher-husband, J.E. Wade. About 1912, she received a visit from her mother's brother, Earl Dalton. He now operated the family dye factory business in London. Presumably he came after not hearing from his sister Ellen for the last several years. Earl loved the excitement of the West, showing a keen interest in the cattle business. For several years he sent a bundle of silk and satin dyed samples that Margaret used to make quilts and pillowcases. The packages and letters stopped coming during World War I (1914-1918).

Emma and Mamie also married and stayed in the greater Lloyd area.

Emma married Carson Carrigan. The same year Mamie married John Barber. Barber was in the cattle business with Wade.

Although both died premature deaths, Ellen and William Thompson left a legacy of several respectable families to the Milk River–Bear's Paw Mountain country. All because Ellen didn't let that first terrible year in that single-room cabin stop her from attaching herself to the Milk River Country.

Two Cattle Queens

Anna C. Callahan, 1861-1950

THE SAME EDITION of the *Chinook Opinion* that told of Ellen Thompson's death and funeral contained the following intriguing sentence on December 11, 1890: "Mrs. Anna Callahan, the cattle queen of the Milk River valley, is in town."

Extensive research turned up only a smattering of information about the woman. Callahan was born in Michigan; her parents were from New York; she had relatives in Canada and her family (by the name of Fernquest) was apparently originally from Sweden. She met a John W. Brown of Oregon and married him, apparently in Seattle, about 1905. They had five children, and she died in Renton, Washington, near Seattle on the south shore of Lake Washington, in 1950. Her husband apparently had died or they had separated between 1920 and 1930.

End of story, almost.

She was known as "the widow Callahan" when she moved from Michigan to the Milk River Country. Newspaper accounts give only faint clues about her. A short-lived column called "Clear Creek Musings" gives us some views of her activities: visiting friends, attending social functions, etc. Clear Creek was both cattle and sheep country, a unique setting in mainly cattle country. The stream ran northwest of the Thompson family's place, flowing into the Milk River near the C.W. Price trading post and the railroad stop of Yantic.

A November 1891 article stated that Anna had hosted a party at her home with dance music provided by the violin of D.E. Murray, with a midnight meal and drinks. Mrs. Callahan went on a trip to the mountains with a W.C. Watts, who had been the "prompter and master of ceremonies" at her house party. A simple shopping trip to Havre rated notice. She also operated the local post office, called Carasco, at her home from 1890 to 1892.

Whatever her activities, she definitely had money and social standing. A story also demonstrated she had pluck, or was gutsy as we would say today. In February of 1892, at the height of winter, Anna was returning from a Saturday buggy trip to Chinook—not a thing women did alone in these days—and stopped to adjust the hand brake. She held onto the reins, but the horses were spooked because of her fur coat and they bolted. She was jerked to the ground, and one wagon wheel went over her foot. She had to walk several miles to the nearest ranch for help in retrieving her rig.

From a fall 1894 article, we know she shipped cattle with the Bear Paw Pool, a group of large-scale ranchers. Perhaps this is about when she sold out to C.M. Jacobs, who later ran a large sheep operation. Like Anna, the Jacobs family hailed from Detroit, Michigan, and the large group she socialized with, either married couples or single women, may all have come from Michigan. A cattle company in the Chinook area, Port Huron Cattle Company, was named for a Michigan town, but Callahan apparently had no connection to it.

She made several trips to Great Falls and Helena, always visiting with "friends" or attending fairs, etc. Callahan made trips to "the East" also, sometimes staying away for several months. At one point, she told the paper she was going to move to Great Falls.

A July 1895 column gives a clue as to where Anna may have lived in Michigan. Nothing that she had stayed at the Chinook House after selling the ranch, the paper listed her hometown as "Tokonha." Unfortunately, no town seems to have existed under that spelling, only a "Tekonsha," located in Calhoun County, where the cereal capital of Battle Creek was the county seat. East of there is the town of Tecumseh, the next closest spelling. (Any mention of her visiting old homes in Michigan, failed to name a town.)

Anna Callahan began visiting Chinook less and less, for example arriving by train from "the East" in July of 1898. On that visit, she took in the Great Falls–Cascade County Fair. Locally, she was a member of the wedding party of Edward Price, "one of Chinook's earliest pioneers and successful business man," and Mary Giblin of St. Paul, Minnesota. The officiating priest, Father Eberschweiler, was a well-known pioneer himself.

At this time, she obviously was still independently wealthy, but there was no clue of the source of her wealth.

She briefly visited Chinook in 1899, 1901 and 1902, then no further mention of her appears in the news. At the end of her final visit, she "departed for Washington [state] to visit friends." Anna returned five years later as Mrs. John W. Brown of Seattle. She spent a week visiting a Mrs. Hanson "and renewing old acquaintances among her old friends here."

The Browns had four children, according to her obituary, but five had been listed on an earlier census. News of her death included no mention of the husband. Two daughters lived in Renton, another in Carson, Washington. A son lived in Inglewood, California, and another in Simms, Montana. Anna had a brother in Canada and another in Sweden. Lastly, Anna had sixteen grandchildren and thirty-three great-grandchildren.

While this writer would love to know more of the Anna Callahan story, the trail has played out. Perhaps one day we will learn more about this wealthy and sophisticated widow from Michigan who left an early imprint on the Milk River country.

Mrs. Nate Collins, b. 1850

Unlike Anna Callahan, Mrs. Nate (Elizabeth Smith) Collins became a national cattle woman phenomenon in the late 1890s. An October 1891 issue of the *Chicago Drovers' Journal* described Mrs. Collins of Choteau, Montana, as the first woman to ship cattle from Montana to the Chicago market, where she sold the cattle for $3.65 to $4.00 per animal.

She explained that originally she and Nate had buyers come to their ranch and bid on the cattle. However, she thought that better prices could be obtained by selling the beeves through the Chicago stockyard. This, the second year of such shipping, found Nate too sick to accompany the herd to the Great Falls rail head, and Mrs. Collins didn't want to trust the herd and the resulting cash to anyone else. So she made the trip alone.

She became famous when the rest of her life story in *The Cattle Queen of Montana*, by Charles Wallace, was published in 1894. A second edition of the book was published in Spokane, Washington; the title was in print until about 1914. (Thirty years later, a feature film was released after being been shot in Glacier National Park, with Barbara Stanwyck in the title role and Ronald Reagan as the male lead—it took nothing but its title from Wallace's book.)

Mrs. Collins was a featured subject in the Montana Exhibition Building, of a world's fair, perhaps the 1893 World's Columbian Exposition at Chicago.

The adventurous life of Elizabeth Smith Collins began in about 1860 when the ten-year-old and her family left Illinois, moving west to Iowa. She and her father soon reached Cherry Creek (present-day Denver), where a mining strike had led to Denver's rise as a mining and agricultural center.

Her father shipped her off to school, but the wagon train she rode with was attacked by Indians—apparently Southern Cheyenne and Arapaho—and she was captured, while all the men were killed. She always bore a scar on her neck where a tomahawk had struck. The chief of these people, "…took a fancy to her and gave her to his little daughter as a playmate." Elizabeth had to witness the torture and death of some of the other wagon train members.

About eight months later, rescuers arrived and the girl was restored to her father. Next she joined her brother on another wagon train, in which she cooked and he drove a wagon. They apparently made many trips as hired help, traveling back and forth from the Rocky Mountains to the southeastern portion of the Missouri River. In her travels, she met a prospector, Nate Collins, and they were subsequently married. However, mining only brought them grief: both broke a leg on the same day, they once had $1,500 in gold dust stolen, and also experienced a flash flood that washed away all their equipment and personal gear. After that disaster, they came to the conclusion that raising cattle might be a safer and more profitable profession.

Sometime before Montana became a state in 1889, they moved to the Choteau area near the Rocky Mountains, which became the headquarters for several large cattle herds in the land between the Sun River, Marias River, and Milk River, after the Blackfeet (Piegan) Indians were removed from these lands in 1873-1874 by the federal government.

Unfortunately, while the ranch prospered, Nate Collins' heart began to fail and Elizabeth had to take over more and more of the operations. After her husband's death, she ventured north to Nome, Alaska, to mine for gold, only one of several gold rushes she participated in.

An article in Fort Benton's *River Press* concluded, "Despite her manlike life, she is still very much a woman, and many a sick cowboy has been nursed back to health by Aunty Collins."

One wonders whether her well-publicized story inspired other women, such as the "Widow Callahan," to come West and try ranching.

Great Warrior of the Gros Ventre Tribal Wars

Red Whip, 1870s

WHEN THE SMALL Gros Ventre tribe ended up surrounded by enemy nations, they fought many battles against Indian peoples in order to preserve their own freedom and culture. In historic times, the great Gros Ventre warrior Red Whip set an example with his honor and battlefield bravery, and became a living legend among his enemies for his powerfully protective war bundle.

The Algonquian-speaking Gros Ventre Indian peoples came to what is now the Canadian province of Saskatchewan perhaps

Red Whip, in 1908

as early as 1700. They settled in the broad prairie basin between the north and south branches of the Saskatchewan River. The tribe had separated from their Arapaho brethren, presumably in present-day North Dakota, who went south to an extensive area between the Yellowstone, Arkansas and Rio Grande rivers. Perhaps their original North American home was the northern part of the present-day state of Minnesota, or perhaps the land between the Georgia Bay of Lake Huron and Lake Ontario, or the lowlands of present-day Manitoba Province or...

Supposedly an anonymous French trader from Montreal saddled them with the tribe name of Gros Ventre (Big Belly), because he misinterpreted their sign language. They were trying to explain they were the waterfall/rapids people. The Blackfoot people added to the confusion by calling them Atsina, the gut people. The tribe eventually became known as the White Clay People—A'aninin—because of white cliffs along the rivers they had inhabited.

The tribe was a small group of about 5,400, but they were as fierce as any other North American tribe. They struggled not to be destroyed by their enemies and such diseases as smallpox and measles, to which they had no immunity. The Gros Ventre were in a precarious position, sandwiched in between the larger, better armed warring tribes of the Blackfoot Confederacy and the Cree-Assiniboine-Chippewa allied forces. For survival, the Gros Ventre and Sarci (Beaver People) allied with the Blackfoot as early as 1808. They faced further enemies to the south in the Shoshoni, Kootenai, Flathead (Salish) and Mountain Crow.

There were wars and wars. Most raiding parties were made up three or four men who went after the enemy to obtain horses for wealth, and personal recognition as brave warriors. Formalized groups of ten or so also went on horse raids. The large scalping parties were usually seeking revenge for an attack against them, especially at an opportune time when small groups of enemies were found.

The Gros Ventre lost several major battles with their enemies, and with diseases that American traders brought up the Missouri River on boats that stopped at Forts Clark and Union. Sometimes an epidemic worked to their advantage, in that some people developed an immunity, allowing warriors to help push their southern enemies away from the Milk and Missouri rivers by about 1800.

About half of the tribal members missed completely one of the smallpox scourges when they traveled south to visit their Arapaho brethren. By this time, the tribe had a bad reputation because of attacking and killing Canadian traders and burning their trading posts. The Gros Ventre felt the traders were being partial to their enemies in selling guns and ammunition.

The southern party had a "good time" trading with the Mexicans on the Cimarron River—and even fighting with the Mexican Army. But the now distinct tribes had a falling out over trading booty, and a chief of each tribe was killed. On their way home, the Gros Ventres harassed traders of the Rocky Mountain Fur Company in the Snake and Green rivers region. Following a major 1832 battle at Pierre's Hole in present-day Wyoming, the Gros Ventre left behind nine bodies, twenty-five horses and all their baggage. The trading party suffered five dead and six wounded, while the tribe was believed to have suffered twenty-three deaths. Presumably this attack took place because of trading with Gros Ventre enemies, the Kootenai and Flatheads. Other Gros Ventre parties were seen, with only one minor skirmish occurring. The groups joined together, and headed north via the Wind River and Owl Creek Mountains to their homelands.

This was not the end of their bad luck, however. When crossing the Mountain Crow territory in the vicinity of the Yellowstone River, they were ambushed by two parties of Mountain Crow in a narrow mountain pass. The Gros Ventre lost sixty-seven warriors, with twice that number of women and children captured. The Gros Ventres retreated from the battlefield, leaving their wounded behind, then had to negotiate for their return.

The same year, a Cree-Assiniboine force attacked a party of Gros Ventre and Piegans who were at the Fort McKenzie trading post on the Missouri River above the mouth of the Marias River. The attack was repelled with the help of the trader's cannon. American Fur Company traders preferred the high quality of the Gros Ventre buffalo robes and beaver pelts, making them an ally of the moment. Incredibly, the same hostiles attacked the Gros Ventre in the Sweetgrass Hills, killing four hundred and leaving only one to tell the tale. This was deep in the Blackfoot people's territory.

The two minor victories in 1835 against the Mountain Crows hardly made up for these kind of losses when the Gros Ventre numbered only about 3,000, with about 1,000 of them warriors. Yet the 1830s through the 1850s was generally a good time for the Gros Ventre. An 1851 treaty was signed making them officially part of the Blackfoot in U.S. government eyes, followed by another in 1855. The Blackfoot Confederacy had regained its strength and northern Montana supremacy after losing two-thirds of its members to a smallpox plague in 1833, having begun with a population of about 18,000 to 20,000.

Of course there were always the Mountain Crow to deal with. The tribes received good manufactured trade items for buffalo robes at Fort Benton. The Gros Ventre still ranged from the Cypress Hills of present-day Saskatchewan along the Milk, Marias and Missouri rivers. They also had the concentrated great northern buffalo herd in their valleys.

This more or less idyllic life came to an end in about 1851 when the Blackfoot Confederacy became an enemy. This couldn't have been worse timing, since a new formidable enemy, the Lakota and Nakoda Sioux, were moving west into their territory.

The incident that finally caused the split occurred when a party of Gros Ventre was chasing horse thieves west from their reservation; the raiding party was Pend d'Oreille from beyond the Rocky Mountains. They left the horses near a Northern Blackfoot camp on the Marias River. Once the Gros Ventre party found the horses, they blamed the northern Blackfoot—and attacked, killing an old chief before they realized their mistake. The Blackfoot Confederacy—particularly the southern Piegans—were already angry because the Gros Ventre had made peace with three bands of upper (Missouri River) Assiniboine and the Mountain Crow. This breach wasn't healed until the 1880s. In the meanwhile, the Gros Ventre, at about 1,080 warriors, was up against about three times that number, not counting the Mountain Crow to the southeast, and the Assiniboine-Cree-Chippewa of Canada.

Now the Gros Ventre were more or less restricted to the Milk

River country, with friendly Assiniboine allowed to hunt in their territory. The River Crow allies were nervous about the Assiniboine, and decided to go south to join their Mountain Crow brethren. Happily the Blackfoot people rarely hunted in that area anymore.

They continued to lose battles against the Blackfoot Confederacy. In one devastating defeat in 1866, the Gros Ventre and River Crow lost three hundred warriors, with three hundred women and children taken prison and nearly all their horses captured.

This occurred in the Cypress Hills, smack in enemy territory. The worst of their losses occurred from 1866 to 1870, when the Blackfeet were also fighting white intruders in their lands. The Gros Ventre tribe was down to 970 members by 1895. Gros Ventre were helped by the shrinking of the Blackfoot (Piegan) lands, with the Blackfoot agency moving northwest to Birch Creek near present-day Choteau, and the Bloods, northern Blackfeet, and north Piegan signed treaties for reserves in Canada. Later the Piegans moved even farther away to Badger Creek near present-day Browning.

In 1866, the Gros Ventre complained to their acting agent that the whites were standing by while the Piegans and Bloods (of the Blackfoot Confederacy) stole their horses and killed them like dogs, and that Canadian tribes and Métis were taking many of their buffalo. The Indian Bureau's answer, two years later, was to put the Gros Ventre–River Crow agency at the Fort Browning trading post near Peoples Creek at the Milk River. True, it put them farther from the Blackfeet, but it placed them closer to the Sioux!

By 1870, approximately 6,800 Yanktonai and Santee Sioux had driven the Gros Ventre and allies out of the Milk River basin, forcing them to retreat south and east to the Bear's Paw and Little Rocky mountains. And, they proclaimed that they had no intention of leaving. In this same period, the Gros Ventre were struck by another major smallpox plague, losing 741 out of 1,200 people. However, other bands of lower Assiniboine, northern Assiniboine and northern Plains Cree often stayed at the agency, bolstering their forces.

Finally in 1871, the Gros Ventre agency was moved east to the new Fort Belknap trading post on the Milk River, south of present-day Chinook. With them were the upper (Missouri River) Assiniboine. Also, the Sioux and lower (Missouri River) Assiniboine were moved to Fort Peck, a trading post on the Missouri River by Dry Creek.

But the year of 1874 brought a bright spot. A Gros Ventre and Assiniboine party defeated a major Piegan force under Black Eagle at Black Butte, just west of present-day Havre and the Beaver Creek Golf Course. Apparently the Gros Ventre/Assiniboine party had left the Little Rocky Mountains for a winter camp on the Milk River, not knowing of the large Sioux force following them. The enemy scouts easily located them, and a dawn attack was planned. The Piegans would have made only a nighttime raid for horses if they had known they now were facing a larger force—others joining near Bull Hook Mountain (Saddle Butte).

The attack began at dawn with the Piegans opening fire on the camp. The war chief Bushy Head rallied his forces, organizing a solid defense. At the same time, the Indian women brought the rest of the horses from the north side of the camp so they could mount a counterattack. The defenders—both on horseback and on foot—attacked from two points, with Bushy Head in front. The Piegans received such heavy destruction that they ran for their lives, leaving their dead and wounded behind.

The defenders now all mounted, and pursued the Piegans east to Indian Women Butte and south to the Bear's Paw Mountains, where the attack was broken off. The following scouts subsequently reported that there were many graves of the wounded, who had died at the Peoples Creek campsite. The Gros Ventre called it "The Place Where They Lost Breech Cloths," because the enemy had run away so fast.

Finally the government was considering a fort in the Milk River country, especially since the last of the non-treaty Lakota Sioux under Sitting Bull, 6,000 to 8,000 strong, were just across the line in Canada, and the Gros Ventre–Assiniboine were still having trouble with the Sioux. Also, large numbers of Canadian Indian tribes were coming south to hunt the last of the buffalo.

Finally, in 1879, Fort Assinniboine was built on Beaver Creek, a southern tributary of the Milk River. At the time it was the second-largest fort in the United States. It's safe to say, it helped save the Gros Ventre from disappearing as a tribe, as did several North American tribes, such as the Mandans. Chiefs Jerry and Little Chief signed a May 1, 1888, treaty agreement, giving the Gros Ventre/lower Assiniboine a reservation of 840,000 acres and a new agency south and east of Harlem, Montana.

The last serious altercation between the Canadian Bloods and Gros Ventre occurred in 1886. A small party of Bloods came to Fort Assinniboine, looking for stolen horses. There they talked to a Gros Ventre war chief. He told them he couldn't help them. On the way home, the six were attacked by perhaps thirty Gros Ventre. The two adults and four teenagers put up a good fight, but all were killed. Finally the great Blood chiefs, Red Crow and Calf Shirts, orchestrated a peace with help of the two governments plus other political leaders.

However, the tribes were not getting enough food from the government. Nor was farming producing a serious amount of supplemental food. When the tribe sold off, for a pittance, the portion of the Little Rockies that had been mined by whites since the 1880s, they at last had a chance to build up a cattle herd, buy tractors, etc. But the money was eaten up by the white bureaucrats.

Loss of the buffalo, disease, alcohol and war had greatly devastated the White Clay People, but the tribe has made a slight comeback to about 5,130 enrolled members, 3,009 of them Gros Ventre. About half of the tribal members live off the reserve. Some progress has been in agriculture, governmental organization, water rights and a tribal college, but unemployment is high, as is on the other Montana reservations where there are no factory jobs.

Life was tough on the reservation, but they still had the memories of their great leaders and warriors, such as Red Whip.

THE GROS VENTRES, to quote historian Regina Flannery, "... are perhaps the least known of the several tribes in the Northern Plains region..." One trouble, she says, was that its long association with the Blackfoot Confederacy blurred the tribe's separate identity. Also there are several accounts of the Blackfeet, while only one major early account survives of the Gros Ventre. It was a paper by A.L. Kroeber, called "Ethnology of the Gros Ventre." The later two-part paper, "Gros Ventres of Montana" by Flannery and Dr. John M. Cooper (1953). is now the bible for Gros Ventre history, culture, and more.

In the 20th century only one name emerged publicly as a Gros Ventre hero—although there were several—and in fact he became a true legend in his own time. "The story of Red Whip's heroic deeds and the great power of his Sacred War Bundle became legendary among the Gros Ventre and many tribes of the plains area, particularly so among the Hunkpapa [Lakota] Sioux and the River and Mountain Crows," wrote J.W. "Duke" Wellington in 1982. Wellington had been the Fort Belknap Agency superintendent until 1954.

Red Whip especially rose to prominence when he was invited to attend the "Last Great Indian Council" held on the Crow reservation in the river valley of the Little Bighorn in 1909. In attendance were all the prominent Indian leaders from around the country. It included a member of the Hunkpapa people, who were a Western-Teton band of the Lakota people or Sioux confederacy, and Francis B. Zahn, an Indian tribal judge, whose grandfather, Flying Cloud, had been killed by Red Whip. He added to the history of Red Whip's great triumph. His and other chiefs' stories were published in a 1913 book entitled, *The Vanishing Race*, by Joseph K. Dixon.

The site of Red Whip's great personal victory occurred a few miles south of the old St. Paul Mission and school near Hays on Montana Highway 66 on the west side of the Little Rocky Mountains.

The battle occurred in the 1870s, when the tribe was settling into north-central Montana between Canada and the Marias, Milk and Missouri rivers. This was in the days when the buffalo was beginning to disappear because of concentrated hunting by Indians, Métis and white hunters. As mentioned, the Gros Ventre were surrounded by several enemies, including former ally the Blackfoot Confederacy, Lakota/Nakota Sioux, Mountain Crow and the Cree-Assiniboine-Chippewa alliance. They still had a tenuous friendship with the River Crows, however.

The battle occurred in early spring. The winter encampment was still surrounded by snow, especially on the north slopes of the coulees and other localities not yet exposed to the sun. The tribe had found plenty of wood, grass and game to survive the winter. Now it was time to journey west or north to the prairies for the spring buffalo hunt.

Eleven young men, members of the Yellowstone River Mountain Crows—believed to have been still friendly—visited the Judith (White) River encampment. Three men volunteered to go with them: one of them was Red Whip, another his partner, Good Strike, and the third was Turtle. Led by a man called Arapaho, they traveled on foot, armed with rifles, knives, and clubs. Red Whip wore his sacred war bundle (one of four), made by a Gros Ventre medicine man named Sun Old Man. Two of Red Whip's uncles, Many Birds Around and Suns His Back, had successfully worn them in combat. War bundles were sacred objects respected by Plains Indians for their great powers.

The party journeyed north and camped on the south side of the Missouri (Big) River in a cottonwood tree grove. In the morning, they followed the river east and crossed at the Cow Creek landing, then moved northeast towards the Little Rocky Mountains until it was too dark to travel.

During the night, Red Whip experienced "a strange and prophetic dream." The dream-like vision took place in the Little Rockies (Fur Caps) to the east. In his dream the mountains were covered with a thick coating of blood. He next confronted a giant buffalo with bright yellow horns. The animal tried to turn the people away and back towards the Missouri River. The dream woke him, and he spent the rest of the night trying to decipher it.

Red Whip told the dream to the others the following morning, suggesting they should turn back and follow the Missouri River east to the Musselshell River, where he had heard a Sioux camp was located. Perhaps, he suggested, there they could steal some horses.

Arapaho, the leader of the Crow party, would not accept the prophetic nature of the dream. He even called Red Whip a coward, suggesting he return to his tribe, put on a dress and be a woman, the worst insult to give a warrior. Arapaho boasted that no trouble would stop *him*. Red Whip made no reply and followed the group northward through the Upper Missouri River breaks. The following morning the party turned eastward toward the Little Rocky Mountains.

Red Whip still believed that the dream was a definite warning and that they should turn back to the Missouri River, only some thirty miles distant. The journey had taken extra time because of the weather, and the caution and stealth involved. He again tried unsuccessfully to convince his fellow leaders, Good Strike and Turtle, that the trip was fraught with danger, but they decided to continue on. Red Whip stayed behind, saying he would catch up with them after smoking his pipe and praying to the Great Spirit for guidance, strength and courage. Two things caused him to go forward and rejoin the party: first, he remembered the power of his war bundle and how it protected his uncles in battle and, second, a golden eagle soared over him; this, he believed, was an answer to his prayer whether to go on or not. He ran at an easy bounding gait and caught the others, with no questions asked.

The party's pace slowed as they encountered the still-snow-bound foothills of the mountain range. They spread out to see if they could spot any buffalo in the immediate area, to kill for a meal. They returned empty-handed to a prearranged spot below a wood-covered ridge. Arapaho ordered Red Whip to climb the ridge to look for buffalo. About a mile away, the latter observed a small herd grazing near the western edge of the mountain slope. He also spied a lone hunter closing in on the herd, hence he called the rest of the party to join him. Shortly they saw a puff of smoke and a buffalo collapse to the ground.

Red Whip couldn't believe that one person would be hunting alone. The rest of his party must be close by. The arrogant Arapaho, of course, disagreed. It was simple, he said, the party would sneak up, kill him and take the buffalo, plus the scalp and personal gear.

Since the hunter and buffalo were in two different coulees, running east and west, Arapaho divided the party into two groups. Red Whip again, for naught, voiced his opinion that the man couldn't be alone. But the men stripped to their breech cloths, put on their war paint, and opened their war bundles. Red Whip painted his body in a yellowish color in accordance with the instructions he received with his war bundle. He then put his otter skin over his head with the otter's head on the left shoulder. Attached to each paw was a bell folded under the skin until used. The warrior also possessed a bone whistle made from an eagle's wing, on a yellow buckskin thong. A small downy eagle plume was fastened to the whistle. The whistle was quite loud, producing an eerie, high pitched and vibrating sound. Also in his sacred bundle were four small buckskin containers of powder designed to stem the flow of blood from a wound.

He was now ready for combat, and he would lead one group. Apparently Arapaho respected the bundle's powers, but not Red Whip. The Crow leader's group had a longer distance to travel. He wanted Red Whip's group to get into position, wait quietly and allow Arapaho and his men to make the kill.

Red Whip's party watched the enemy warrior as he made a purification grass fire for his hands and rifle, thanking the Great Spirit for allowing him the kill. They waited impatiently for Arapaho's group to arrive, but in the meanwhile Red Whip unwrapped the bells and readied his whistle.

Finally they heard Arapaho's war whoop, and they charged

the lone hunter. The desperate man attempted to escape, running toward the thick timber, but Red Whip, who was ahead of his group, shot him before he could disappear. Red Whip then "counted coup" (touched his enemy) and took his scalp. The now-combined party concluded he was Sioux by the beaded design on his clothes. They also hungrily ate some raw buffalo meat, because Arapaho nixed building a fire. He, too, was beginning to worry that the dead man might have companions, even though he wouldn't verbally acknowledge that Red Whip might be right.

And, sure enough, a party of about one hundred Lakota Sioux appeared from behind a high ridge, heading toward them. The Crow leader, paralyzed with fear, now followed Red Whip's directions. Red Whip and his companions fought a delaying action while the Crows headed back to a washout with three to four high, snow-filled banks. Red Whip constantly charged the Sioux, blowing his whistle and shaking his bells. The Sioux had heard of this powerful war bundle and the possessor painted in yellow with blue spots; they concentrated their fire on him, but to no avail. Yellow Hawk, a noted Sioux leader, told the 1909 assembled North American Canadian Indian leaders at the Last Great Indian Council, that trying to shoot Red Whip, "...was like trying to hit a blade of grass in the wind."

Although the Gros Ventre party made it to the coulee, Sioux marksman killed several of their party and seriously wounded Good Strike. The Sioux suffered several losses, and they would have been satisfied to withdraw from the battlefield—if they could kill Red Whip. They hope to engage him in hand-to-hand combat. However, he turned the tables by charging them! Red Whip repeated his attacks into the enemy ranks until the Sioux retreated a fair distance. One Sioux warrior did make it into the coulee, and approached him from the rear, except at the last second Red Whip turned and shot him down.

The battle was over.

Good Strike couldn't walk because of a broken leg and its accompanying profusely bleeding wound. Good Strike begged Red

Whip to leave him, giving him his personal possessions for his mother, and instructions that included never giving his horse away, taking care of his mother, and telling her of the great battle. They sang the Gros Ventre war song, and he told Good Strike to sing it until the end. Red Whip kissed his life-long friend and ran to catch up with the others, which he did in late afternoon in the Missouri River Breaks. Six Crows were also left behind because of their debilitating wounds.

Now Red Whip had his turn to castigate Arapaho and his companions for their cowardice. He told them to return to their village since they were no longer welcome at the Gros Ventre camp. He warned his companion, Turtle, that they dare not camp any more with the Crows, because the Crows would kill them to cover up their cowardice. The next morning, the two lagged behind and hid in a deep coulee. Once they were certain the Crows were gone, they journeyed to Fort Claggett trading post at the confluence of the Missouri and Judith Rivers where they received meals and food for the trip home. The Gros Ventre regularly traded at the post, so they were well received. The traders were also able to direct them to their new encampment on the Marias River, where they arrived the next day. Red Whip and Turtle returned to their village as heroes, and told of Good Strike's heroism in battle and in death. He also gave Good Strike's mother the sewing kit and broken mirror, plus the little bay horse, which she could never give away. He told her that he had taken an oath to watch over her.

In the evening, Red Whip and Turtle told the whole story of their battle, including the cowardice of Arapaho and his followers. And too, Red Whip displayed the scalp of the dead Sioux leader, Flying Cloud.

The many Sioux deaths and other casualties were corroborated by both Gros Ventre and Lakota (Teton) Sioux historians. It indeed was a positive chapter in the war history of the Gros Ventre.

And the medicine bundle? It became the property of Wellington after he transferred from Fort Belknap to the Standing Rock Sioux Agency in North Dakota. It was presented to him by Phillip Shortman, a tribal elder and brother-in-law of Red Whip, in compliance with the wishes of Tribal Chairman Rufus Warrior (circa 1957).

THIS WASN'T THE ONLY record of Red Whip's activities. He served as a scout for "Bear Shirt"—otherwise known as Colonel Nelson A. Miles—during the eastern Montana campaigns against the Lakota (Teton), Northern Cheyenne and Northern Arapaho, during the winter of 1876-1877. Miles commanded his troops during this portion of the Great Sioux War in engagements at Ash Creek, Bark Creek, Cedar Creek, Muddy Creek, Spring Creek and the Wolf Mountains.

At the time of Red Whip's involvement, Miles commanded the Fifth Infantry Regiment, which had left Fort Leavenworth for the Yellowstone River country after Custer's devastating defeat at the Battle of the Little Bighorn. In that 1876 fight, the Seventh Cavalry lost five of twelve companies. Miles established a temporary post (cantonment) at the confluence at the Tongue and Yellowstone rivers, building a permanent post, Fort Keogh, there the following year.

The colonel's vigorous winter campaign uprooted the Lakota (Teton) Sioux of eastern Montana: part returned to or went to reservations in the Dakota Territory, and part fled to Canada under Sitting Bull and other prominent chiefs. The latter 6,000 to 8,000 people ranged between the Wood Mountain Northwest Mounted Police post and their headquarters at Fort Walsh, both in the present-day southern Saskatchewan province.

Red Whip didn't give the name of the battle in which he participated, but he said that it occurred near the Tongue River, southwest of the military post. He said it was a long fight in which many died on both sides. Furthermore, he stated that the exhausted troops temporarily retreated from the battlefield, taking back their wounded soldiers. After a rest, Red Whip said, the troops returned to the battlefield "...and had another long fight and fought until sundown." This time the troops held their ground and camped (bivouacked) overnight. The next morning the fight commenced again, and the conflict lasted all day, until the Sioux retreated. Red Whip said he helped collect the dead soldiers' bodies and buried them on the battlefield. He then accompanied the soldiers back to the Tongue River cantonment. From there he went home.

This story was believed to have been told at the council in 1909, when Red Whip was old, which conceivably accounts for the fact that this story doesn't conform exactly to any of Miles' recorded battles. Only two battles come close to his description: The Battle of the Wolf Mountains and the Battle of Muddy Creek. In the former, Miles' troops had just returned from skirmishes near the Missouri River trading post at Fort Peck, a favorite hangout of Sitting Bull. The trip involved severe weather conditions of ice storms and drifting, deep snow, and those troops were still exhausted. This battle occurred against Oglalas under the great Sioux warrior Crazy Horse, and the Northern Cheyenne under White Bull and Two Moon.

To raid this camp, the soldiers of the 5th and 22nd Infantry regiments had to be dressed in heavy gear, including buffalo coats, arctic overshoes, face-masks, canvas leg grips, etc. This made walking much tougher and combat more dangerous. They marched up the Tongue River Valley until the Indian scouts made contact on New Year's Day, as the troops continued toward the Wolf Mountain village at Deer Creek. When temperatures moderated, the men, their horses and wagons now struggled through snow, ice and mud.

Finally, on January 8, the scouts stumbled onto the main body of hostiles, being surrounded by them on three sides, waiting atop steep ridges. After a ferocious all-day battle, the Indians withdrew, carrying the great Cheyenne medicine man, Big Crow. The combination of artillery, poor visibility, and shortage of ammunition prevented the usual Indians' mode of attack. However, casualties were minimal, with only one soldier killed and none wounded, and perhaps four Sioux and Northern Cheyenne warriors killed and three wounded. The army finally cut off their pursuit because of low supplies.

The last major battle occurred at Muddy Creek, an eastern tributary of Rosebud Creek against a body of Minneconjous Sioux on May 7, 1877. The attack by the 22nd Infantry and 2nd Cavalry against their village occurred in the early morning. The Indians suffered fourteen deaths, including that of Chief Lame Deer, and four soldiers were killed with nine wounded. In the deserted camp was found "many trophies of the Custer battle and several scalps of white men and women." Also in their large horse herd were horses with the 7th Cavalry brand.

The Battle of Muddy Creek and the death of Chief Lame Deer concluded the major battles of the Great Sioux War; however, skirmishes continued against the Sioux from Canada whenever they roamed into northern Montana to raid and hunt. The troops from Fort Assinniboine, Fort Buford and Fort Keogh kept the latter and his people contained until his surrender in 1881.

Red Whip probably appreciated being involved in the fall of the Lakota (Teton) Sioux and allies, who had terrorized the Gros Ventre in earlier years.

If he were alive today, Red Whip would probably urge the young to not forget their history, but also to get an education to compete in today's world. In fact, one of the education facilities at Fort Belknap Tribal College is named after him.

Travels of an Outlaw's Widow
Elfie Dessery-Logan, 1878-1965

FOR OUTLAW HISTORIANS, the remote Landusky mining, horse and cattle raising region of northern Montana, overshadowed by the Little Rocky Mountains, is of prime importance. Not only was it known for former Wyoming gunslingers as well as gold, it had been the home of the tall and rangy Powell "Pike" Landusky, who came from "Pike County, Missouri, by God!" (his preamble to knocking opponents flat and stomping them into submission).

Also it was known for the "Curry" brothers, transplants from Missouri via Wyoming and perhaps Texas or Oklahoma. They ranched on Rock Creek south of Pike, and had a mysterious ranching partner called James Thornhill. The four became two after one lost a gunfight and the other died of TB. For several reasons, including brother Lonie's infatuation with Pike's stepdaughter, Elfie, they became enemies.

Landusky, from St. Louis, landed by steamboat at Fort Benton in the Montana Territory when the fabled gold strikes began in 1862 near the soon-to-be prosperous towns of Bannack, Virginia City and Helena, now the capital. Pike worked, drank and fought his way through being a miner, Indian trader in the greater Judith River and Judith Mountains country, cowboy, rancher and finally one of the prominent gold discoverers and mine "owner" on Gros Ventre Indian lands. Not to leave out town founder and liquor merchant.

Landusky married a French divorcée with five children, named Julia St. Denis (or St. Peter). One of the children was Cinderilla

Athanissa Dessery, known as "Elfie." They moved north from the mining town of Maiden, Montana, to live in a dugout until Pike and his partners could find the mother lode.

At the height of Pike's career and wealth in 1894, he engaged in a no holds brawl and gunfight with the younger, smaller but husky Harvey "Kid Curry" Logan. Logan equaled Pike in nerve, fierceness and strength. Logan's killing of Landusky set him off on an outlaw career that would be unparalleled. His is most associated with the "Hole-in-the-Wall" gang, and the "Wild Bunch"; the latter prominently included Robert LeRoy Parker, "Butch Cassidy," and Harry Longabaugh, the "Sundance Kid."

Logan's most famous local robbery occurred on July 3, 1901 west of Malta, Montana, at Exeter Creek, where he robbed the Number 3 Westbound Great Northern Railway passenger train. He collected $40,000 in unsigned currency, eight gold watches and a bolt of silk "for his old lady." In the robbery process, he blew up the express car, wounded two railroad men and a young female passenger. Logan and his two partners, O.C. "Deaf" Hanks and Ben "The Tall Texan" Kilpatrick (and possibly his girlfriend Laura Bullion) escaped without a trace returning to San Antonio, Texas, before going on separate tours of the East and South before being captured.

The National Criminal Investigation Bureau in 1910 described Logan as having had the longest criminal record in the United States and that he had accumulated rewards of $40,000 for his crimes of murder, robbery, rustling, et al.

The killing of Pike left his widow Julia with a family and a Landusky–Rock Creek ranch to run. The death of Harvey's brother Lonie at the hands of Pinkerton agents and law officers in Kansas City, Missouri, also left Elfie a widow with two small children: Mayme and Lonie Jr. (The nickname, pronounced with a long "o," was shortened from the given name "Lorango.") The Pinkerton Detective Agency was the main force pursuing the train and bank robbers of the West.

The Pinkertons were on Harvey's trail in late 1901 when he

went on a tour of the South with his girlfriend, Annie Rogers. At that point the "Wild Bunch" was no more and "Butch" and "Sundance" were on their way to South America. Logan escaped from the Knoxville, Tennessee, county jail in 1903, and it set off a nationwide manhunt. It seemed to the Little Rocky Mountain–Landusky area residents that there was a Pinkerton man behind every tree and rock. Even when it was believed that Harvey committed suicide after an aborted train robbery near Parachute, Colorado, in 1904 they still checked—just in case.

Perhaps they paid particular attention to Elfie, who was the only connection the area had left to the infamous Currys. Her visits over the years to the Landusky area were akin to celebrity sightings. And, too, perhaps she held the key to what really happened to Harvey "Kid Curry" Logan.

While the reports of Harvey's sightings in the West were driving the Pinkerton brothers crazy, the Little Rockies and Landusky were virtually forgotten as far as the outlaw period was concerned. Besides it was nice to be able to walk down the mining town's streets without ducking bullets. The *Fort Benton River Press* commented that, "the rough crowd at Landusky is gradually being killed off, and there is good prospect of peace in that section in the near future." The gold mining industry in Zortman-Landusky continued to grow, thanks mainly to the Ruby Gulch Mining Company. They expanded, taking in mines to the east and west of the Zortman area. The mill operation was enlarged in 1907 with the additional mines. Fire destroyed that operation in 1912 and a new 600-ton cyanide-processing mill came into existence in 1914. Yes, it looked good for the mining future of the Little Rockies.

Life for Julia Landusky and daughter Elfie Logan didn't look as bright, however. They both had lost their husbands to gunfire, and they had children to care for. Elfie lost the Harlem rental home when Lonie left Harlem to escape from the Pinkertons, and Lonie had sold their saloon for getaway money. Elfie returned to the Little Rockies where she took employment as a servant and hotel employee of the John Ellis family. Ellis was a former Texas cowboy who had been at the town and Missouri River steamboat landing Rocky Point before buying his new hotel business in Landusky. Elfie's children attended school at St. Paul's Mission at Hays on the Fort Belknap Indian Reservation. The fee was ten dollars a month that she tried paying unsuccessfully with the Rock Creek–Wilcox train robbery money Lonie had given her. With Lonie dead, her job gone in June 1901 since the Ellises abruptly moved on, she had no reason to stay in Landusky. She arranged to have daughter Mayme left with the Paul and Mary Sunday family in Havre, and she took Lonie Jr. on the road with her. Apparently she had no desire to stay in Montana because she immediately left the state. (Perhaps she was afraid of being indicted for passing the money.) Bill Hart, Chinook friend and former business partner of Lonie's, gave her two hundred dollars, which he claimed he owed Lonie. Elfie used part of the money to go to Kansas City, presumably to visit sister-in-law Arda "Allie" Logan and her family, besides viewing Lonie's grave-site. Their son called him "Oney Turry."

Next, according to her self-recorded history, she went to Roff, Oklahoma, southwest of Ada in Pontotoc County. This is where brother-in-law James and his wife Mattie were living. Elfie worked in a dining hall of a hotel operated by "two old maids." She said the cook used to get drunk on vanilla extract, and the mother of the sisters had to do the cooking. Logan apparently got along with the women, except for having to eat in the kitchen. However, she didn't agree with their policy of recycling food left on patrons' plates. But the job paid well, so she accepted the working conditions. The women also helped her make clothes, including her underwear, although they thought it scandalous because the 21-year-old put lace on them.

Her next known place of employment was at Oklahoma City where she put Lonie Jr. in the Shawnee Sisters School. Brother-in-law James and Mattie had separated, and she lost a place to stay. Her traveling costs were apparently low because of the railroad pass she received from railroader father, Victor Dessery. The boy suffered a broken arm at the Oklahoma City mission school; it was the same one he had dislocated at St. Paul's. Next she moved on to Marshall, Texas, located near the border with Louisiana, across from Shreveport. Again there is no mention of her occupation, but it certainly had something to do with food service or hotel work and not dance hall work, as one historian claimed. The Sisters of Charity convent school required a uniform, she recalled.

The northern Montana newspapers gave us the next mention of her travels. Elfie arrived at the Harlem train station on July 20, 1904, and she journeyed to Landusky where she said she would spend the rest of the summer visiting friends. In September she left for Boise, Idaho, to visit friends, then went on to southern California to spend the winter. It is not clear whom she knew in Boise or California, or for whatever reason, if this was even the truth. She might have run into former brother-in-law Lee Self, but not on her next trip because he died of a heart attack in 1913 after exiting a Landusky saloon. Self had been married to Allie Logan. After their divorce, Allie moved to Kansas City and re-married.

The next town mentioned in her dictated memoirs was Portallis, New Mexico, in the mid-eastern part of the state near the Texas border. We only learn that she spent about two years there. From Portallis the journey continued, as she traveled to Spokane, Washington. She procured employment in the city and sent for her son. Elfie said that Lonie Jr. had lost his cap and lunch. A girl of unknown age watched over him, and where he got the cushion he was holding over his head wasn't explained. She enrolled him in a Catholic school, but that didn't work out, so she moved him to the Huston private school.

WITH ELFIE AND SON in Spokane about 1908, it's time to catch up with her mother Julia and family. Julia had a ranch to take care of besides the cattle that was on government-leased land. She apparently had trouble getting anyone to work for a woman, therefore she and the children had to bear the brunt of the work. However, that didn't work out either. Her sixteen-year-old son, Charlie Landusky, had become a juvenile delinquent, or "dead hard" as the Justice Court judge of Harlem put it. Young Landusky had refused to obey his mother and was "a general nuisance to his neighbors at Landusky." The general nuisance charge included stealing horses from the nearby Fort Belknap Indian Reservation. He had joined his eighteen-year-old brother, Bennie Landusky, in that thievery. For that, he was shipped off to the reformatory at Miles City. Bennie presumably received jail time. It seems surprising that neither Julia's married children, or friends of hers and Pike's wouldn't help out. Julia proved up the land in August 1899, and later sold it, but she realized little profit because of the $10,250 owed to the Mission Peak Mining Company and others, from Pike's dealings. She suggested that the Landusky estate money was lost for other than honorable reasons.

Unfortunately, Julia's memoirs next jump to 1926, leaving many years to piece together.

We do know she and her two Landusky sons moved to Washington State. Julia apparently married a Grant McGhan, following him to a new gold camp. The local papers announced in 1904 that "Mrs. P. Landusky had relocated to a pleasant resort at Bolster, Washington and is getting along splendidly." The booming gold mining town was in the Meyers Creek mining district, about two miles south of Okanagon County. The Lewistown paper claimed Julia had bought a Cuban plantation, but that information can easily be discounted.

She is next heard of in May of 1906 when she returned to the Little Rockies for a visit. Former Logan brothers friend and partner, Jim Thornhill, and wife Lucy hosted the Landuskys, with side visits to Havre and Chinook. The next newspaper report occurred in February of 1907, carrying the tragic news that her older Landusky son, Bennie, aged nineteen, had died of diphtheria at Bolster. Julia at the time was in Spokane with her daughter Mrs. Tim (Lollie) Maloney. When she returned to Bolster, she found Charlie, two years older, was severely ill with the same disease.

Julia's third husband, McGhan, supposedly died the same year, perhaps from diphtheria.

The Public Lands records show Julia moving to Waterville, Washington, south of Bolster, on land east of the Columbia River, in Douglas County. She bought 242 acres of federally administered land. The next documented leap is to 1936 in the Los Angeles County, although there is some confusion by 1909 about whether she traveled with Elfie and lived in Richland, North Yakima and Seattle before moving to California. Her son Charlie lived in the area of Compton, Placer County, California, according to the 1920 census, and in Roseville, Placer County, in the 1930 edition. Lonie Jr. also lived in Roseville. Julia died in Paradise, Butte County, California, in 1945 at the age of ninety-two. She had had at least one other husband, but had none at the time of her death. She moved to Paradise because daughter Elfie had lived there since about 1935. What attraction the town had is unknown, although it was a former gold mining area, located in the foothills of the Sierra Madre—perhaps reminding them of Landusky. Lonie Jr. also moved to the town in 1959, after retiring from the California Highway Department.

Now back to Elfie in her roaming days after 1909. The Huston school was working out well for her and about ten-year-old, Lonie Jr. until he and the teacher's son broke out school windows on a dare from some older boys. Both women had to pay for the damage. Elfie at the time was living at a mining town in British Columbia, Canada, apparently called Phoenix. She apparently operated a restaurant. British Columbia has a vast mining region of many minerals except gold, but gold was a by-product from copper smelting. The town and mountain of Phoenix was located in south central British Columbia near the principal town of Grand Forks. The mine and smelter closed in 1919. It was not that far from Bolster, WA.

Lonie's schooling became a problem again when the Huston school closed, and the teacher, Mrs. Hitchcock, put him and her son into the Lyons school. About this time (1910) Elfie returned to Havre to find out what had become of the Sundays. Her last two money-order letters had been returned "address unknown." In later correspondence between Mamie and Elfie it is learned that Mamie and the Sundays had left Havre for Spokane, where they owned a hotel for three years. They sold it and moved to Tacoma, and then on to Seattle and finally back to Great Falls in 1916.

Since Elfie could not find any trace of the Sundays, she decided to attend the Fourth of July activities in the Little Rockies. She said they had a good time, probably again staying at the Thornhills', since her mother and boys had also hit the road. Lonie Jr. even won the apple-bobbing contest. It was probably great fun for both of them, because they had spent so little time together in recent months. Of the people who were not friends or acquaintances, Elfie noticed them whispering about her being the widow of the notorious outlaw Lonie Logan, and how the boy looked like him. Through a Millie Tressler Wolfe, she found a possible person who knew the whereabouts of her mother Julia. The Dan Tressler family had owned the Winter-Gill ranch. His ex-wife, Lucy, was now married to Jim Thornhill after being involved with Johnny Logan. The narrative ended at this point.

It is believed that Elfie did catch up with her mother, although it would be several years before they reunited with Mamie. From a postcard, we know that Elfie put Lonie Jr. in a Catholic school in South Park (S. Seattle, WA) and she returned to the city in 1910. In the latter part of 1910, she heard from her nephew L.B. Orman, only the note was addressed to her under a new married name. Bob Orman had been a partner of Pike Landusky, having married Pike's stepdaughter Alice.

Elfie married an Englishman, Wallace Budden, who managed a hotel in Seattle. The 1920 U.S. Census lists Budden's age at thirty-six, Elfie's at forty-one. Lonie, then twenty-one, lived with them. Apparently she knew Budden from her British Columbia days. They had previously lived in Portland. At some point Elfie returned to Portland, and apparently moved to California in the mid-1930² to join her mother and brother.

BACK IN GREAT FALLS, the Sunday family had settled in their new home. Besides having a boarding house, Paul worked as an electrician for the Great Falls Electric Company at the hydroelectric dam. Sunday had worked for the Havre electric plant before moving to the Pacific Northwest. Sunday died at forty-six when there was an accident while he was loading machinery for Burch and Son bridge and building contractors. His body was returned to Delano near Minneapolis. Mary also eventually returned to Minnesota.

Mayme "Mamie Della Rae" Logan married Eugene B. Moran in 1916 at the age of eighteen. Moran was an accountant for an oil company. The company wanted Moran to transfer to Shelby, but he promised Mamie that they would stay in Great Falls, requiring him to find other work. His jobs included hauling coal, working at the smelter and finally at the Montana Flour Mill, maker of Sapphire Flour; he worked there for many years. The couple had five sons and two daughters. Except for Leo, who died in Great Falls, and Sharon, who lives in north central Montana, the rest of the family resides in California.

An important event for Mamie occurred in 1931. She finally found her mother and grandmother. By then Elfie had left both Washington state and Oregon behind, moving initially to the Sacramento area. Through being referred by a woman in Great Falls, to a family in Jordan, Montana, and finally to a member of the Dessery family at Bonner's Ferry, Idaho, she was able to find both Julia and Lonie Jr. She had believed they were both dead since she couldn't find any trace of them. She explained in her letter about leaving Havre with the Sunday family, for cities in Washington state, before returning to Great Falls. She wrote of having had been married for fifteen years, and stated that she had six children.

She gave their names, ages, and a little about them, moving on to talk about her husband—"I have a good man"—and his job at the flour mill, where he had worked for eight or nine years. She asked about Lonie Jr., whether he was married and how he was doing job-wise. With this contact the family came back together. Lonie Jr. even lived in Great Falls for a few years.

In September of 1933, the family reunion took place. Mother Elfie and Grandmother Julia drove up from California in a Model A Ford, picked up Mamie and headed for Landusky. Mamie hadn't seen her mother in twenty-seven years, and perhaps Julia even longer. They visited all the old haunts, including Pike's grave and the former Logan brothers ranch. They camped out under the Big Sky, catching up on many years.

The *Great Falls Tribune* correspondent for Landusky, Johnny Ritch, did an article about them for the newspaper. In that interview, Julia, age eighty-one, she said it was her first visit in thirty years, and she noted the loss of many of the old landmarks, especially their old ranch buildings just below town. The long-vacant Landusky "ghost" house had been torn down and moved away by a farmer to build a new house. At Pike's grave, Julia defended him, saying the old stories about his being a brute and a bully were not true. She also said that the killing of her husband (by Harvey) was cold-blooded murder.

Julia was not around for the next visit, due to her death in 1945 at the age of ninety-three. Elfie and Julia had moved to Paradise, California, about the same year of 1936. Besides Elfie, her daughters Lollie and Julia also lived in California. Lonie Jr. moved to Paradise in about 1959, having retired from the California Highway Department. He had honorably served in World War I in the U.S. Navy.

Eugene Moran died in 1958 from an automobile accident. Mamie moved to Lincoln, Montana, having a cabin built on the Seven-Up ranch outside the town. This is where the couple planned to retire, although they had talked about moving to Seattle at one time. Since son Don was the only single one in the family, he commuted to Missoula while staying with her. She lived only a few years, suffering a heart attack in Great Falls.

Elfie's last trip to Landusky occurred in July of 1957 when she was seventy-eight years old. She was accompanied by one of her sisters. They introduced themselves to Ted Duvall and they discussed the local history, over lunch with Duvall and his wife. As Julia had, she commented on how many more buildings were gone that she was familiar with in earlier years. Specifically the old Pike Landusky Saloon where Pike had died and burned down. Pike would have had fits if he knew it had operated as the Kid Curry Inn! They visited the graves of Pike Landusky, Johnny Logan and Jim Winters. In their two-day stay they spent several hours with Bill Kellerman who had been brought west by Pike Landusky. Elfie had quite a crush on him at one time.

She spoke before the Little Rockies Historical group, saying that many lies had been told about the Logan boys. She said that she had been able to get a television show stopped in California because of the untruths it included. She also told them that she disliked James Horan's book, *Desperate Men*, and its portrayal of the Logan boys. They finished their trip by going to Harlem, where Lonie and Elfie had lived, and Lonie and first cousin Bob Lee had briefly operated a saloon.

The last visit of Elfie's was the most important to some Wild Bunch researchers. She was talking to Ruel Horner, who had come to the Little Rockies in 1903 and was the last of the local stage drivers between Zortman and Malta. Horner had also been a miner, and worked as a cowboy for the Circle C, Phillips and Hensen ranches. Horner was quoted in a 1959 *Great Falls Tribune* article of Sunday, November 22, that Elfie said, "the Kid Harvey died of injuries he had received in a car accident in the state of Washington not too many years ago." Former Chouteau County deputy sheriff John Buckley said that the local residents know even more: that Harvey died of that accident in a Seattle hospital. There is a tradition in the Logan-Moran family that such an accident occurred in the 1930s. The senior Moran brother and his wife witnessed Elfie burn a trunk load of materials before moving to a rest home. She was overheard saying something to the effect that now nobody will ever find him. Whatever secrets she held, they went to the grave with her in 1965.

SHARON MORAN AND her dear friend Earl Hofeldt, thought they could put the whole matter to rest by having "J.H. Ross" dug up at the Glenwood Springs cemetery to compare family DNA, but the old plot records no longer existed and there had been landslides on the cemetery hill. Ross was the name the Parachute train robber was buried under.

Hence no one has ever refuted Pinkerton Agent Lowell Spence's contention that Ross was Harvey Logan, although the mismatched scars remain an issue. Brown Waller's book about Harvey Logan states in the end, "If it were not Harvey Logan who was buried in a train robber's grave on Grand River (now the Colorado) at Glenwood Springs in the ageless Colorado hills, the outlaw codes of the Old West certainly keep their secrets well."

For the Logan-Moran family, it was precisely their tradition that Harvey left the outlaw-life after escaping from Knoxville and the secret was kept. That tradition, however, still is unproved.

Milk River Angel of Mercy

Thora Fremming Phalen, 1873-1958

AT THE TURN of the 20th century, northern Montana offered very few luxuries, or even all the basics of life, such as medical care. Havre, then a rough-cut boardwalk shanty town, was no different. It was blessed with two well-qualified doctors in Duncan Mackenzie and Joseph Almas, although a hospital was years away, and rural care was basically non-existent. Health care was "Root, hog or die," as the expression went. The Chouteau County seat at Fort Benton, some seventy-five miles away, possessed the nearest hospital, and the larger city of Great Falls lay forty miles beyond. At least, trains could get you there, as well as on to major U.S. cities.

Late in 1901, Thora Fremming and a nurse friend decided to take a Great Northern Railway train from St. Paul, Minnesota, to the west coast city of Seattle, which suffered a scarcity of nurses. Fate would soon change their plan, however. Their

Thora Fremming, probably in 1897.

train stopped at Havre due to a train wreck west of town. The two decided to tour town since they were grounded for a few hours.

They entered a different world that abounded in wild cowboys, rough single railway men, coal miners, and loitering off-duty U.S. Cavalry soldiers from nearby Fort Assinniboine. Many of the men's horses were tied to the hitching rails in front of the businesses, mostly saloons. At the train depot were American Indians, perhaps of the Plains Cree tribe, wrapped in blankets and dealing in polished buffalo horns—sometimes mounted on scrap wood and cloth—beaded belts, moccasins, and more. Since the fort no longer provided casual work for these former nomads, they had collected buffalo bones from the vast empty prairies to be transported by rail back east for commercial purposes. The bones were soon gone and the horns were all that remained.

The front display windows of Stringfellow's drugstore on the main street caught the nurses' eyes, with "all the then widely used nostrums such as 3-H liniment, peruna, Lydia Pinkham's [highly alcoholic] remedy, hair tonic, CCC pills and calomel." Proprietor Henry Stringfellow tried his best to persuade the women to stay in Havre since nurses were badly needed. Seattle was a greater lure with its boisterous boomtown atmosphere because of the major Klondike gold strike in the western Yukon Territory of Canada. This had turned Seattle into a major seaport overnight.

Soon the railroad tracks were cleared and the two were on their way, but only about three miles' distance. A fellow female passenger's baby needed fresh milk and the galley had none. Thora, nurse that she was, bravely walked across the "hostile" prairie and visited a nearby ranch. She met Mrs. Mike Healey, who supplied the milk for the infant. Thora was both impressed with the western hospitality and unimpressed with the uncompromising and harsh-looking prairie country.

This would be the end of our story, except that Thora's respiratory system couldn't continue with the humid, rainy weather of Seattle. She must find a drier climate and higher-altitude country, her doctors told her. Hence she returned to Montana, but this time a more mountainous region, staying with a sister, Sophus, on a homestead near the state capital at Helena (4,124 feet about sea level). The country proved ideal. However, Thora's new job at St. Peter's Hospital put her right in the middle of a typhoid epidemic, which broke out during the early phase of construction at the Hauser Dam on the Missouri River, east of Helena, in 1905.

Shortly after this, she and a cousin visited an uncle who was then living in the Bear's Paw Mountains area, thirty-five miles south of Havre. Thora was surprised to see that the rough and ready town had survived a major fire, and now sported the beginnings of modern brick buildings. The town had electric lights, telephones and other modern conveniences. Great Northern Railway magnate James J. Hill was happy that the old cowboy town had finally calmed—at least on the surface—and he could at last attract married men to work for his Havre passenger-freight-maintenance railroad complex.

The journey to her uncle Matt Staff's ranch on Clear Creek took the cousins south through the Beaver Creek Valley, east over the divide to Sucker Creek, and farther yet over the Little Box Elder Creek divide, where they stopped at the Nick Faber ranch. There they had lunch before traveling on to her uncle's place.

Events took a sharp turn for Thora when, by the following spring, she had found herself married to a Bear's Paw rancher and had become a "horse-backing nurse." It wasn't quite that simple: she returned to Helena, but there must have been a lot of mail going back and forth with Ambrose Phalen before the couple was married in Helena.

The tall, long-legged and slender Ambrose was one of several brothers who came from Ontario, Canada. He told his family back home that "the country was so vast and rugged it would never be settled. You'll have the world by the tail," he exclaimed.

The two met when Thora first visited the Staff ranch. Phalen stopped for lunch on his way to Havre for medical attention. He had injured his hand, and home remedies hadn't stemmed the subsequent infection. Thora's doctoring of the wound led to romance and Thora's settling as a rancher's wife in the mountain wilderness. It was said it took a person with a dose of "grit, guts and gusto" to contend with this country. Was the city girl up to it? Yes. In fact she far exceeded the minimum qualifications.

The woman described as a "tall (5'8") willowy brunette with Nordic blue eyes" had traveled to the shores of America in 1894 from Oslo, Norway, at the age of seventeen. Accompanying Thora were seven younger sisters and a brother. They settled in St. Paul, Minnesota, where an older sibling already resided. Thora's first job was picking berries, but soon she became a nanny/housekeeper for wealthy families, where she learned English from their children. She successfully passed the entrance examination at the city's Ancker Hospital, and she graduated from the nursing program in 1897. Her previous education in Norway compared favorably to a college liberal arts degree of today, she stated. In 1898 she became one of the first U.S. Army nurses to serve in Cuba during the Spanish-American War, where she was the equivalent of an Army second lieutenant. She returned to her former hospital employment after the war.

In St. Paul, she worked with the physician-inventor of a type of sterilizer, and also learned to make the first catgut suture used by surgeons. These were considered important medical achievements of the time. There she would have probably lived out her life if fate hadn't intervened in the person of James J. Hill, founder of the Great Northern Railway, who suggested the Seattle employment idea.

But this was all behind her as she settled in to the Milk River–Bear's Paw Mountains country between Birch and Clear creeks. However, if Ambrose Phalen expected his marriage to Thora to give him a simple, well-regulated life, he was badly mistaken. For she would be in demand as a nurse twenty-four hours a day, seven days a week. Soon the farmers, ranchers and other area residents for many miles around would know that a nurse resided there.

About a year and one-half later, Thora became the administrator of the local Havre–Chouteau County poor farm, located about three miles west on the Theodore Roosevelt Trail; it paid twenty dollars a month. Obviously Thora was the best pick, being the only nurse in the area. And, too, the ranching business in 1906-1907 had taken a bad turn, with dry, hot summers and frequent heavy winter snowstorms killing the already emaciated cattle.

Coincidently, the poor farm sat on land previously owned by the Michael Healey family, including the wife who had provided the fresh milk for the baby on Thora's westbound train. So Thora now resided in the house she once had described as dark and gloomy, a place where she would hate to live, but it was spacious with seven rooms. Chouteau County acquired the 100-acre site for $6,000; half the land was under cultivation, farming implements included. Residents raised vegetables and chickens, and collected eggs—the surplus sold on the Havre area market to supplement county funding.

The residents' needs included everything from childbirth assistance to senility care. Four special, small, frame buildings on the adjacent south hills housed the smallpox cases and other people with contagious diseases, while the main two-story facility held everyone else. Heating and lighting came from coal and kerosene delivered from Havre, along with ice. The county furnished these necessities, and provided all necessary repair work.

The main building had six steps to the first level, making carrying water from the nearby well, or anything else, a major chore. The swamp-like land had necessitated a higher than usual building. This building later became the first men's dormitory on the Northern Montana college campus. The adjacent Healey cottage became the Phalens' home when they had time to enjoy it. As Thora said, "I had fine training for marathon racing."

One problem was cleaning up newly arrived residents, especially sheepherders. She used coal tar to remove their layers of dirt acquired during the warm months. For this purpose, the building contained a room with a tub on wheels, a washbowl, a stove for hot water and a small mirror to show what clean looked like.

Besides the hibernating sheepherders, they also housed veterans of the American Civil War. One veteran in particular, "Charlie," had been shot in the head, and he had a plate that could easily be removed to show his brain matter. Charlie and another inmate constantly argued, making the Phalens believe they had fought on different sides of the conflict.

The Phalens had two other veterans, of the Spanish-American War, mules Jack and Sam, to assist them. These two animals provided dependable transportation to town and back, besides not being bothered by the noises of Havre—including gunfire. Thora herself seemed to take the vice district in stride, an area including Christopher "Shorty" Young's pleasure palace complex and seventeen other saloons she had to pass by. Thora found herself fascinated by the antics of "Ma Plaz" (Alice Pleasant) who came and went from the barrooms, bumming both cigars and drinks. The two-hundred-pound black woman was the only woman tolerated at the gaming tables.

Ma Plaz had her restaurant nearby on west First Street, specializing in scrumptious southern fried chicken and steak. Another Phalen whom considered an excellent chef was a man named Osborne, "who would serve a steak out of this world." Pleasant and Osborn both came from the environs of Fort Assinniboine: he as restaurateur in the post trader's complex, and she as the wife of a soldier, perhaps initially working as a laundress, but reportedly later owning a soldiers' "hog ranch," or low-class brothel, on Beaver Creek with another woman.

It is doubtful that either of those local characters had to suffer the same long hours of drudgery as residents at the poor farm. And the work situation became worse when Thora injured her arm, then neglected it because she was so busy. It became badly infected to the point that it wouldn't bend.

For aid, she probably went to Doctor J.S. Almas, a town doctor and health officer. Although an excellent doctor, he always delighted in assuming a gruff manner until his victims had been thoroughly awed. Then he would laugh and become quite friendly. Phalen first met Almas at his office. The doctor was working with a young patient whose foot had been seriously cut by an ax, "Bring your damaged carcass inside so I can look at it," he told the boy's father. While Almas prepared a hypodermic needle of sedative medicine, Phalen removed the makeshift bandages and assisted him as he sutured the foot, left a drain and bandaged it. After finishing, Almas asked, "Who in the hell are you?" He soon learned what a great nurse the area now had. Presumably they saw much of each other when he regularly inspected her facility.

However, he couldn't help with the damaged arm, and she went to doctors in St. Paul. The arm, though, was now damaged beyond medical expertise, and she returned home. To regain any use of the arm, she had Ambrose break it and set it in a bent position so she could have partial use of it and the fingers.

The Phalens stopped managing the poor house in 1912, when Hill County became a reality, with Havre as the county seat. They settled on a ranch at Warrick, on the south side of the mountains. Warrick gained a post office in 1890, originally for and at the NL Horse ranch near Birch and Dog creeks.

The ranch, one of the highest in the mountains with some of its summer range atop Old Baldy Mountain, prospered under the Phalens' care. They bought several adjacent properties as owners either gave up or couldn't pay their taxes. The Phalens fenced in an additional eleven homesteads.

Returning to an isolated area that had no medical care placed her and her husband right back in a medical war zone. One writer said that here Thora's life "as a pioneer nurse began in earnest." Apparently he had never seen a county poor farm.

According to Earl J. Bronson, then retired Hill County clerk and recorder, who wrote many fine articles about early Havre, "Expectant mothers put the greatest demand on her and with no consideration for time and weather." Since she rode horseback from ranch to ranch, the first article of clothing to replace was her riding skirt, which had a nasty habit of catching on the saddle horn. Ambrose told her to "take the damn things off." Jeans then became standard attire—a first for a local woman. In the winter, she was unrecognizable in the many layers of clothing including canvas leggings, sheepskin overcoat, woolen cap with ear-flaps and as she said, "about everything I could find [to wear]." Not only did she minister to the sick or pregnant, she also cooked and cleaned for them.

The local doctors, such as Almas, D.S. McKenzie, and P. O'Malley, were more than happy to give her support, including medical supplies, since they would not have to leave town so often.

Thora and Ambrose never knew minute to minute, day or night, when a rider would pull up to take her to some emergency situation. Sometimes the patient came to her, as when the neighbors brought an expectant mother, bed and all, to their bunkhouse in below-zero temperatures. The winters were the worst, with Thora having to ride barely visible snow-covered trails, or go over alternate routes of deep snow-filled ridges broken up by thiniced creeks. Sometimes they had only a fence line to guide them and on occasion she had to attend to her own frozen fingers, nose and face. Sometimes her trips were nearly back to back.

Phalen was also on the cutting edge of delivering transverse (crosswise) fetuses, something a doctor hoped he would never confront. Breech babies were bad enough. That process required Phalen to administer enough anesthesia to completely relax the skeletal muscles, but not harm the baby or mother. Once she determined the baby's uterine position for delivery, she rotated the child into the correct position without damaging the placenta or harming the children's lower body. As Dr. Volney Steele exclaimed, "What an amazing feat for a nurse alone in the backwoods of Montana."

At the Chris Rhue ranch, Thora faced the birth of premature twins, Olga and Emma. They weighed only one pound apiece, according to the kitchen scale. Through the night Thora kept one baby warm by placing it under her clothing, while the mother cared for the other. She improvised with the stove's warming oven, making an incubator of sorts. Three days later she went home, confident of another success.

In another long, winter rescue trip, she went to a sick child in an unheated shack where wind was blowing through the flimsy walls. For water, she heated some snow, wrapped the child in blankets and made her a bed with wood piece she found in the yard.

Somehow, she raised three children, kept up a house, made sure her children had an education, knitted and read in her "spare time," and the Phalens even hosted weekend dances. She also was enthusiastic about politics and equal rights, embracing the views of Belva Ann Lockwood, American lawyer and civil rights activist.

The number of babies delivered by Thora Phalen from 1906 to 1929 is anyone's guess. Perhaps two hundred is an accurate figure. What is known: she was there when she was needed and she never said no.

Perhaps her greatest challenge came during the "Spanish" influenza, or grippe, pandemic of 1918, apparently begun by World War I veterans returning from Europe. Sacred Heart Hospital of Havre and St. Clare Hospital of Fort Benton were overwhelmed. Other towns used hotels, opera houses and meeting houses as hospitals. Pneumonia added to the deaths, with only ice packs for fever relief. Whiskey, brandy and raw eggs became a common home remedy. Sick beds filled up as fast as the dead were removed.

To add locally to the mass misery, the rains ceased and crops failed. And with the end of the war, the government ceased the farm-products support program.

During the flu scourge, Thora Phalen went from ranch to ranch, homestead to homestead treating the sick as doctor, nurse and housekeeper/cook. She claimed to not have lost a patient, while about 500,000 persons died in the United States alone.

Thora became a widow herself when Ambrose died in an automobile accident in 1932. Now in her seventies, Thora moved to Havre during World War II and worked at the Deaconess Hospital as a nurse supervisor. Son John took over the family ranch. Thora stayed active, belonging to the Havre Business and Professional Women's Club, Montana State Nurses Association, the Lutheran Church, Hill County Republican Central Committee, Havre Chamber of Commerce and the Assinniboine Camp #12, Department of Montana United Spanish-American War Veterans, its only woman member and the first to head the camp. Her most prized honor came as a service commendation from President Dwight D. Eisenhower.

Thora died at her daughter Janet's home in Havre at the age of eighty-five, in December of 1958. When feeling ill, she made her way to the sofa and called her daughter. She said "Come sit down beside me. Hold me tight. I'm going now"—and she died. The day before she had made out her Christmas gift list for her daughter to shop with, and meticulously checked items against the list later in the day.

She was buried with military honors next to her husband in the Chinook cemetery.

As a eulogy by Earl J. Bronson concluded, "...Mrs. Phalen was indeed one of the pioneer women of this territory, serving her community in any capacity when called upon and always giving it her best." He left out exceptional, proud and independent. Another version of this is 2 Timothy 4:7-8, "I have fought the good fight, I have finished the race, I have kept the faith. Amen."

Journeying to & Living at the Fort in the 1880s

Mary Kellogg

THE BISMARCK (Dakota Territory) *Tribune*, beginning in 1879, detailed the building of Fort Assinniboine in north central Montana Territory, along with the initial troop and supply movements from train to steamboat at Bismarck and by wagon from Coal Banks Landing to the fort. One of their correspondents at the fort building site was Mary Wickham Kellogg, wife of senior Captain Edgar Royme Kellogg, U.S. 18th Infantry Regiment.

The troop movement began from McPherson Army Barracks

The paddle-wheeler Rosebud *in port, viewed from the stern.* MONTANA HISTORICAL SOCIETY PHOTOGRAPH ARCHIVES, HELENA, MT

in Atlanta, Georgia, in April of 1879. Two trains with double lo-
comotives were used, one for baggage, the other for the officers,
families, servants/cooks, enlisted men, laundresses, civilian workers, etc. Also aboard were some of the prospective post traders,
who hopeful for the lucrative contract for supplying goods and
services. The passenger train consisted of eight passenger cars and
two sleeping coaches, while the baggage train pulled eighteen cars.

At the Bismarck Missouri River port, three rear-paddle wheel
steamboats awaited the trains: *Far West, Josephine* and *U.S. General Sherman.* Soon the first two boats were tightly packed with
people, while the *U.S. General Sherman* carried the horses, mules,
ambulances, wagons, and other freight, and the boats departed
for the 450-mile trip, destined for the lands of the Gros Ventre,
Blackfoot Confederacy and River Crow.

Mary and her two daughters, Lizzie and Lucy, weren't at Bismarck that April of 1879. Hence she avoided being on the passenger train that the *Tribune* described as not having "any space
thrown away." However, husband Captain Kellogg was among the
officers on the *Josephine.*

The couple would give a view into their river travels and the
fort because of Mary's connection to both the *St. Paul (MN) Pioneer* and *Norwalk (OH) Reflector.* Mary at sixteen had helped
operate the family paper during the American Civil War when her
three older brothers enlisted, and her father was elected a member
of the Ohio Senate, resulting in his temporary move to the state
capital of Columbus. In her memoirs she wrote, "I learned to do
many things thought only suitable for a young man, such as mail-
ing, collecting, setting type and even feeding the [printing] press."

She met Edgar when he stayed at his brother's home in Norwalk to recuperate from wounds he received at the 1864 Battle of
Jonesboro, the last battle of General Sherman's Atlanta campaign.
They married in February 1866, and she became an army wife.
The move to the Montana Territory was their first trip into the
"wilds of the West," as she put it. At that time Edgar was thirty-eight, Mary was thirty-five, and the two daughters four and

five. No mention was made of son "D.W.," who was thirteen; however he does show up on fort rolls in June 1880.

Mary both wrote and shared part of her husband's letters from their separate journeys. In Edgar's case, the steamer convoy's first stop happened at Fort Stevenson, above the Knife River, some 110 miles northwest of Bismarck. The smaller *Josephine* joined the other two boats already docked. The crew and passengers enjoyed a good-natured race between river ports, though Kellogg's boat was smaller and slower.

Kellogg's letter introduced the country where the new fort would be located, giving Fort Benton, the Missouri and Milk River's and Bear's Paw Mountains as the focal points, with the smaller streams described in between. Kellogg also wrote of Chief Sitting Bull and the large party of western Lakota Sioux defiantly camped on Frenchman's Creek, instead of their safe haven in Canada. He expressed in writing the opinions expressed of the new lands, varying from being "a horrid country" to being "an unearthly paradise." Kellogg concluded he was sure it would be a great country, since so far it was "a delightful trip."

He went on to explain the final landing port would be at Coal Banks military landing, about forty miles from the new fort and twenty-five miles from Fort Benton. Once there, one company of soldiers would be left at the landing for the summer to guard the supplies, as the multiple following boats arrived. Furthermore, he said that only six companies of soldiers would remain the winter, since all the living quarters could not be completed in time. Instead the remainder of the troops would march southward to other military posts, including Fort Shaw, Fort Ellis and old Fort Logan.

At the time, there was still a national interest in the final military drive to conquer the non-treaty Sioux, who had wiped out more than half of Colonel George Custer's 7th Cavalry command at the Little Bighorn River in southeastern Montana.

Kellogg probably was the one who reported to the *St. Paul Pioneer* of the ambush/battle between the arriving troops and a force of unknown Indian tribe, situated on Square (Box Elder) Butte where "...several Indians were killed." The military wagon train had just broken camp, preceding north on the last few miles to the building site. It was not known until a later date that they were Plains Cree, who were considered British-American subjects, and not wanted on the already designated Indian lands of northern Montana.

Apparently the summer was going smoothly for Captain Kellogg; at least there were no shared correspondence to the contrary. The original plan called for Kellogg's family to spend the next year at Norwalk with her parents until Assinniboine's first living quarters were finished in the fall. However, she received a letter from Edgar to leave immediately for Montana during the "June rise" when the Missouri River was usually at its fullest. The wife of First Lieutenant George Hoyt was to accompany her, but couldn't be ready until August, when they would meet in Chicago for the railroad trip to Bismarck. Kellogg in turn sent his "stryker," as Mary described him, back on the *Red Cloud* with passes for the two families. Usually a striker was a soldier/servant, but in this case the man named Cunningham was thought to be a civilian military maintenance worker from the fort.

Unfortunately the plan failed temporarily because the *Red Cloud* didn't appear on time at Bismarck, and their hotel bills were mounting, leaving them no choice but to book passage on the *Rosebud*. The *Rosebud* departed with 160 people on board, forty of them being crewman. The average size of those flat bottom boats was 252 feet in length with two engines, three wood-burning boilers and two engineers to tend them. The pilot house rose about 85 feet in the air and was a favorite visiting spot for passengers. Carrying 500 tons of freight was common for these steamers that drew only three feet of water.

Unfortunately, this would not be the pleasant cruise her husband enjoyed, since the river water had dropped dramatically.

About two days out from Bismarck, early in the morning, they heard an exchange of boat whistles. They rushed out on deck to see the *Red Cloud* going by; on deck was Cunningham, helplessly watching them. She first assumed that he had left the army and was going home. Cunningham was able to debark a short time later probably when they stopped for wood, and rented horses. He caught up with them after riding continuously day and night. She wrote in her memoirs that the poor man "was so groggy and unsteady from having been in the saddle…," that she at first thought he was drunk.

Uniting with Cunningham didn't change their luck, though. The high "June rise" was gone by August, causing their boat to bog down on sandbars, and rarely did the water measure the necessary three feet. This condition worsened after they passed Fort Buford, when they lost the voluminous downstream flow of the Yellowstone River, which entered the Missouri near the fort. They almost lost Cunningham at the small military post when he went ashore, seeking fresh provisions, and the boat continued the mile or so to the former site of Fort Union. This time he was without the benefit of a horse.

The western Lakota Sioux had kept this post constantly under siege until Colonel Nelson Miles and his troops cleared the hostiles during the winter and spring of 1876-1877, after the Battle of the Little Bighorn. Nowhere in her memoirs does Mary even mention seeing unfriendly American Indians, but she wasn't prone to writing about unhappy military subjects.

The next stop she mentioned was the trading post, Indian agency and sometime military camp, Fort Peck. The low river-level had required them to "double trip" most of the way. From twin upright stationary booms (beams), which pivoted at the base, were attached telephone-pole–length spars controlled by a rope and pulley system and run by an auxiliary engine. The spars were set in the sand near the bow sides and pointed downstream with the main engines going at full power. The spar system allowed the boat to "leapfrog" ten or so feet forward.

Mary said the auxiliary engine ran at such high pitch the passengers had to yell at each other to be heard. Finally one of the spars broke between Forts Buford and Peck, causing crew members to search for a replacement tree log—in a country of few trees. After the first proved too small, a larger diameter tree had to be found. This episode probably cost them a day in travel.

The nights added another dimension: for light a large wire cage hung from the bow, filled with burning pine. The snap, crackle and pop its pitch caused, combined with the flying sparks covering the boat, gave the passengers a bizarre sensual experience.

Added to their misery, the supply of fresh water gave out; also the meat supply. The meat problem was solved by the thousands of buffalo crossing the river in front of the boat. The killed animals were hauled aboard with blocks and tackles, and dressed by crew members.

The boat stopped near Fort Peck on August 18 just nine miles short of Fort Peck, apparently stuck on an extensive sandbar. The Peck officers, from Colonel Nelson Miles' command, lacking female company, eagerly came to call. Mary wrote that she and Mrs. Hoyt "found comfort in their encampment." They received a real treat of precious lemonade, but raisins for the children were passed by, in case they were spoiled. The children found their treat in inspecting the officer's tents, enjoying what they contained. At departure time, some officers gave the ladies each a pair of chickens so they would have eggs now and at the fort.

Mary again didn't record the Sioux War's status. However, she must have been told about the major battle that took place with Sitting Bull's forces the previous month near the Milk River and Beaver Creek. She did record that they learned the river was at its lowest level in about eight years.

Before reaching the next main port of Fort Claggett—a former military post and now a Power Brothers of Fort Benton trading post, near the mouth of Judith River, they stopped at two points, probably at the Musselshell River and Carroll landings. To reach either point, some freight had to be offloaded, and then reloaded downstream once the offending sandbar was conquered.

Power Brothers workers were concerned whether the boat could even make it beyond Claggett to Cow Island, much less

Coal Banks Landing, about 8.5 miles distant. Their fears were confirmed when another spar broke just short of Claggett Landing. A violent prairie rain- and windstorm added to the passengers' misery. Conditions were so perilous as the boat was pummeled that passengers stayed in their day clothes and life preservers all night. Towards a calmer morning, one of the Power Brothers staff headed for Fort Benton to get assistance, including a new spar and replacement provisions. In the meantime, trading post employees worked on unloading their cargo.

During this time, Kellogg and the other officers waited at Coal Banks Landing, worrying that no word had been heard from the two-weeks-overdue boat. Finally he and an unidentified sergeant set out in a skiff to try to locate the steamboat. They tried to sail through the night, but the storm was too fierce and they paddled ashore. At first they didn't want to attract any hostiles by lighting a fire, but they finally decided pneumonia would be worse. Once at Claggett, Kellogg sent the sergeant back to Coal Banks Landing to bring the wagons up, since the low water stopped any further travel by steam.

The Power Brothers relief party with boats and wagons finally arrived, unloading the *Red Cloud*, and providing the passengers with provisions.

Captain Kellogg was now at Claggett, anxiously awaiting transportation to the steamboat. Cunningham decided to learn the army's whereabouts, hiking to Claggett with the Kellogg girls. On return, the girls told their mother of seeing their father there. Mary was in disbelief, but no, they insisted, it was their papa in his blue military trousers. Cunningham confirmed this, and they were shortly reunited. Soon the spar was replaced, and the lightened boat made it to Claggett, where army wagons now awaited the military wives. About twenty other passengers decided to join the military caravan for the security of its military escort, having gained Captain Kellogg's permission.

In her memoirs, Mary wrote vividly of the spectacle of twenty rushing people commandeering horses and three wagons from the boat—even an open lumber wagon—then pulling quilts and blankets from the berths for wraps, and seizing anything they could find from the pantry. The lunch break finished off these meager rations, but Kellogg supplied them with additional food and hot coffee. The convoy continued through the night, trudging on against the storm until they reached Coal Banks in the morning. The ladies' chicken coop cargo from Fort Peck, placed on top of the baggage wagon, even survived.

Awaiting the travelers at the landing were a doctor, sheltered warm fires and presumably warm food and drink. The doctor gave up his tent for a particularly "delicate looking young lady," who was going to the Sun River country to teach school against her family's protests. The fires soon dried the travelers' clothes.

This next morning brought no letup in the rain. The teamster told Kellogg it would be impossible to get up the slippery, mud-coated hill without going at least five miles around it. Kellogg had to order the wagons out, since the teamsters did want to even try the detour.

Because nothing further of the trip is described in Mary's writings, it would be a good guess that she and the children slept soundly all the way. She did ask her husband to wake them near the fort if need be. The children had consistently asked if they were "there yet" on the train ride between Norwalk and Chicago. She had explained no, but said that when they arrived, she would say, "Thank you, Lord." Edgar did awaken them when he saw the dim light of the distant tent village, and she told them, "There is Fort Assinniboine, thank the Lord." Since no telegraph lines had been constructed yet to Coal Banks or Fort Benton, poor Lieutenant George Hoyt spent every extra moment standing on the lookout of the (old) post stockade to catch sight of the wagon train.

Mary thought the tents with wooden floors were "very comfortable and commodious," and who wouldn't have after the five-week trip she experienced? She also appreciated an officer giving her a pair of curlews he had just hunted, even though the meat left much to be desired. She concluded the day's happenings with,

"Soon after I retired, the wolves began to howl and I felt as if I certainly was in the wilderness."

Hannah McCulloh

Mrs. Robert L. McCulloh (Hannah Elizabeth Blanchard), wife of co-post trader at Fort Assinniboine, also told of her adventures traveling in the wilds to Fort Assinniboine. Unlike Mary Kellogg, Hannah told her story in brief to the *Kansas City Star* in April of 1931, when she was in her seventies and living at Lee's Summit Missouri. She then was in her thirteenth year of widowhood.

The young Mormon girl living in Logan, Utah, married McCulloh, and she moved to Corinne, where her husband worked for the Diamond R Transportation Company. The company's main depot forwarded freight from both the Western and Union Pacific railroads north by bull train across eastern Idaho, through Fort Hall where the Oregon Trail intersected, and across the Continental Divide at Monida Pass. At the end of the 450-mile trip stood Helena, the company's northern depot. From there, freight was delivered all over Montana and as far north as Fort Benton, to connect with the river boats. As the Utah and Northern narrow gauge railroad snaked north, following approximately the same trail, its main headquarters eventually moved to Helena, the gold rush capital of Montana, conveniently located on the main north-south trail.

The McCullohs were probably quite happy in Helena in comparison to the hell-on-wheels town of Corinne. The log and canvas town quickly blossomed into a civilized, rich town of splendid brick and sandstone buildings and homes. When Charles Broadwater returned to Helena, McCulloh left the company's bank and took over its post trader operations.

Hannah followed him twice: once north in a stagecoach to Helena, and by sleigh to Fort Assinniboine some three years later.

The stagecoach ride north on the Montana Trail for a young woman and her one-year-old son Edgar was as good as any in a western movie. It was comforting that another mother with a girl about Edgar's age rode with them. Hannah didn't, however, take comfort in the stage's gold bullion cargo, which was accompanied by several guards. She'd heard that several coaches had been robbed in the Portneuf River Canyon they were approaching. In one of those holdups, the passengers died violently.

Just before the canyon entrance, south of Pocatello, Idaho, the coach stopped, and the guards dismounted. One of the bandits, who served as lookout, lit a signal fire to signal the rest of the gang to prepare for a coach. But, this time, the guards made sure the fire *and* the outlaw were extinguished. They did pass the other gang members at their holdup location, but those bandits weren't ready when they faced the guards with weapons drawn. Mrs. McCulloh noticed ripped-open mailbags and their contents scattered all over the ground. She probably took the scene better than most, since she experienced hostile Indians early in her life around Logan.

From there until Helena, we suppose she faced nothing more than the usual bad roads, some with sheer drop-offs or hills requiring the passengers to walk temporarily, poor food, and the lack of sleep in the cramped coach—along with complaints from unhappy and sick children.

Hannah's trip to Fort Assinniboine a few years later occurred during the worst of winters, with blizzards, extreme cold, and a trail blocked at times by snowdrifts. She joined a military payroll detail led by a Major Arthur (brother of President Chester Arthur), she proudly explained, on it way to Forts Shaw, Benton and Assinniboine. The temperature registered minus 54 degrees when the party started out. The trip in good weather took ten days, and accompanying would have been her surviving son, Carroll, and younger half- or stepsister, Idonia Blanchard.

The sleighs were apparently too light, as they turned over at any serious snowdrift. The passengers' snow-filled clothing felt colder than the outside air, Hannah explained. A few times they came close to being trampled by the mules. Except for the spills, the trip to Fort Shaw on the Sun River was uneventful until they reached Birdtail Divide—where an invasion of warm chinook winds from the east slopes of the Rocky Mountains turned the trail into a mixture of mud in deep, snow-filled ravines. At Fort Shaw, they switched to wagons for the trip to Fort Benton on the Missouri River. Sometimes it was necessary for the passengers to walk because of the steep hills being covered with deep snow, when all the teams had to be utilized to pull one wagon at a time. On one of those occasions, Hannah walked too close to a wagon wheel, getting her scarf caught and pulled tighter and tighter around her neck. She gasped, "choking" before she passed out. Fortunately she was revived without any injuries except a major gash on her cheek.

The chinook winds ceased as they neared Fort Benton, and their world froze again, requiring a switch back to sleighs.

Soon they saw the Bear's Paw Mountains in the hazy distance, signaling perhaps thirty more miles to the fort. Just ahead, at the Big Sandy Creek crossing, stood the store/warehouse operation of Broadwater's other partner, C.J. McNamara. Somewhere closer to the mountains they saw dark specks in the snow, which turned out to be a stranded young newlywed couple, in a wagon beside a fire. The couple already had burned two of their wagons for warmth and signaling. They happily joined the caravan. Hannah said another day of exposure and the pair would have died.

Meanwhile, at the fort, a patrol had been sent out to look for the overdue party.

As night fell, the sleighs continued on the path they thought led to the fort, but actually they were going away from it. They were saved when the sleighs again overturned, and their screams attracted the patrol, which arrived on the scene minutes later. Soon they were in the safety of the fort, instead of facing death.

Leisure Life at Fort Assinniboine

HANNAH MCCULLOH agreed with Mary Kellogg that the fort's leisure life made up for its harsh winters, saying that the McCullohs, post officers and their wives became a small social group of educated persons surrounded by the wilderness. "The enjoyment within his wilderness," she said, "seemed to be hers and the chosen few." Their festivities centered around the officers club—women admitted once a week—the officers amusement hall, individual officers' own quarters, and the post trader's home.

Since Mary Kellogg had grown up in an "affluent illustrious family" with schooling in social graces, the arts, etc., it would be interesting to know what she thought of the officers who came up through the ranks and were married to former laundresses or servants.

This companionship included formal dinners with eight to ten courses, with the best of their combined silver, crystal, china and linen table cloths and napkins; formal and informal dances with the post band providing the music, amateur theatricals, card parties, ice skating, ice sailing, and so on. In the warmer seasons the group picnicked at Beaver Creek in the shadow of the Bear's Paws, and enjoyed horseback rides and polo games, hunting, and tennis, plus sporting competitions against the enlisted men, including baseball, football and field events. Sometimes the group attended social events in Fort Benton or Helena as well as going shopping. Sometimes officer couples from other forts joined the shopping expeditions.

Mary Kellogg especially enjoyed weekly visits to the officers club, where the women were allowed to play billiards. The three-times-a-week mail and newspapers delivery from Fort Benton was always looked forward to, all items being read over and over again. The group needed little excuse to have a dinner party: birthdays, anniversaries, Department of Dakota or Helena headquarters inspectors or commanding officers and the paymaster from Helena. Also, "quarters dinners" and card or quilting parties happened on a regular basis. As she could, Mary wrote letters, and articles for the newspapers.

Mary did remember that the arrival of dashing First Lieutenant John J. Pershing perked up the social events. Pershing frequented the Kellogg quarters, often visiting with her younger sister, Idonia. Although their relationship was not allowed to bloom, they remained longtime friends.

Another activity Mary enjoyed was cooking. She became quite inventive in supplementing the usual beef or pork roast with native duck, breast of prairie chicken on toast, and jellies made from local berries. She placed them in special "beer bottle" jars, the bottlenecks removed through a heating and cooling process. She was quite pleased when visiting Montana commander Colonel Rujar complemented her on her jelly.

Trips to the mountains were another popular activity. These overnight stays involved many support people, such as a soldier escort and teamsters with wagons. A Quartermaster Corps sergeant set up a canteen near their creekside tent city. The soldiers hauled trout to the chosen creek from creeks on the east side of the mountains.

All these activities would not have been possible with her now three daughters, except that the family had a nurse, cook and handy man: "Aunt Susan," "Aunt Jane," and "Uncle George," all from the South.

Other than expressing pleasure at moving from the tents into the first-officers duplex in the fall (Edgar was senior captain), and

Fort Assinniboine's administration building, with the fort still under construction around it. Montana Historical Society Photograph Archives, Helena, MT

how hard it had been to keep dust and dirt out of the tents, especially when cooking meals, or the dangers of cooking in a tent, she still didn't write about the fort's military operations.

Throughout her first summer at Assinniboine, a large construction crew of soldiers, government civilian workers from St. Paul, and Red River Valley Métis, labored through a very hot and dry season, under a fierce mosquito presence. Quarrymen mined limestone from the nearby east hills for foundations, and other men contended with the brick kilns as the brick-molding machines spat out thousands of bricks. Other excitement included a mid-winter expedition of all the fort's forces sent east to Frenchman Creek when Sitting Bull's force again appeared, the major prairie fire that almost reached the buildings, and frequent firefights with parties of Plains Cree attacking or stealing from the reservation Indians.

Only what affected Mary's personal life rated mention, but one story about forty frostbitten soldiers was an exception. Another personal instance involved Edgar on a routine hunting trip to the mountains, accompanied by a Lieutenant McClare and an unnamed soldier. The hunting party left the fort early on a clear winter's morning. Upon their return trip, late in the afternoon, a blizzard struck. With little visibility, they wandered around lost for eleven hours. Kellogg tried his best to keep them on a northeast line to the fort, using the technique of keeping the wind blowing on his right cheek.

The fort's commander had sent out a search party of Gros Ventre scouts, who returned empty-handed. The head officer then ordered a bonfire built on an adjacent hill to guide them in. Finally the hunters saw the flames in the distance. They arrived at the bonfire, warmed up and tried to figure out exactly where they were. It was now 2:00 A.M. Looking around, they discovered a telegraph pole, and literally ran into the second one. They were now on the fort grounds, but could not see the buildings through the blinding snow. Finally they followed a light, which led them to the (old) stockade, and received an escort to their quarters. Mary, Mrs. Hoyt and the post medico, Dr. Percy, were waiting.

Later Mary learned that the Hoyts had decided to take her in if Kellogg was dead, since she would immediately lose her quarters. The Hoyts planned to escort her to Fort Benton in the spring, for the steamboat ride back to Bismarck.

The regiment left Montana in the spring of 1885, its main force assigned to Fort Leavenworth, Kansas, while Captain Kellogg went to Fort Hayes, Kansas. Mary spent the summer with her parents in Ohio, rejoining him in the fall. While Mary hated the northern Montana winters, she did miss the modern, spacious quarters that were lacking at their next two posts.

Later, Edgar's assignment to Cleveland, Ohio, presented new challenges. With no fort, there was no automatic delivery of necessities like wood, coal and ice.

The Kelloggs saw many forts and cities, and their daughters married officers. Kellogg contracted "jungle fever" in the Spanish-American War and never really recovered. Daughter Elizabeth lost her husband in that war, and he never saw his new baby. Edgar Kellogg retired in 1899 as a brigadier general; his career had begun as a private in the 24th Ohio Volunteer Infantry at Camp Chase, Ohio, in 1861. He died at their permanent home in Toledo, in 1914. Mary wrote her memoirs from that city, sometime in the 1930s. Her family encouraged her to record them, but by then her memory was not at its best; however, her old newspaper columns helped jog her memory. Granddaughter Kate ended up with the hand-written manuscript, and her niece Betty planned to type it. That never happened, but the handwritten copy, happily, was preserved.

The "Lost" Marias Pass

John F. Stevens and His Search, 1889

IT DIDN'T APPEAR, in 1883, that the Minneapolis, St. Paul and Manitoba Railway would go farther west from its new terminus at Devil's Lake, Dakota Territory, near Fort Totten; this was only some ninety miles west of the Minnesota state line, at the Red River. However, Montana territorial delegate Martin Maginnis, and leading citizens Paris Gibson and Charles Broadwater, had different ideas. The northern railroad was needed to gain access to the Indian lands for white settlement, to exploit the mineral wealth between Great Falls and Butte, and to develop the falls of the Missouri River and their adjoining Great Falls town site. James J.

Hill, though, saw too many obstacles. First, the Northern Pacific Railroad had already entered Montana through southern, accessible passes; second, the Panic of 1884 made money scarce; and, third, the expense of building west from between Great Falls and Helena through the mountains was too high.

This didn't stop the Montana men, however, and they persuaded Hill to join them for a tour of the country.

John Stevens at the 1925 dedication of his statue atop Marias Pass

145

They rode, camped and talked with Hill. He warmed up to their idea, seeing that bringing the rails west along the Milk River and then south would solve his problem with the southerly Northern Pacific Railroad. The combination of the water-power potential at Great Falls and the vast coal reserves in the Sand Coulee area, not to mention precious metals, was too much to pass up.

So, a plan was formulated over a campfire to build a local Montana railroad from Helena to Great Falls, connecting it to the main Great Northern Railway line once that was built along the Milk River. The 197-mile line came into being in the summer of 1881 with Charles Broadwater as president. It was a railroad in name only, with its tracks to be laid by Hill's "Manitoba Road" crews once they entered north-central Montana.

In the meanwhile, Hill had to convince President Grover Cleveland to allow him access to land through the Indian reservations at Fort Berthold, Dakota Territory, and across northern Montana. The bill became law in February of 1887. Now Hill had to negotiate the sale of the needed reservation land at a fair market value. To prepare for Montana Road construction, the Great Northern built 117 miles west to its newly established western terminus at Minot, Dakota Territory, named for Henry Minot, the railroad's acquisitions manager.

The following summer, Hill's graders, roadbed builders and track layers laid 643 miles of track, averaging five miles per day and reaching Helena on November 18. The 6,600 men, with 3,000 teams of horses, moved over 10 million cubic yards of soil. Each 30-foot-long rail laid weighed 600 pounds, and thirty-six 200-pound kegs of spikes were used per mile. The following year, they constructed the more difficult stretch from Helena south to Butte.

Hill already had shares of stock issued for the Great Falls Water and Light Company, Red Mountain Coal Company and Montana Central Railroad, keeping a majority, of course. He also established a temporary western headquarters two miles north of the protective Fort Assinniboine. This complex housed an office, depot, roundhouse and section house. And he continued to expand his easterly operation in the upper Mississippi River–Great Lakes region, and acquired lake-going steamships.

Now all Hill needed to complete his railroad to the West Coast was to find the legendary lost Marias Pass—and hope came in the form of a young Great Northern construction engineer named John F. Stevens.

By November, the winter of 1889 brought a bitter, bone-chilling cold and the Rocky Mountains already were blanketed in heavy snow.

Stevens set out from the Post Trader's Store at Fort Assinniboine, near present-day Havre, now the western terminus for the Great Northern, on his urgent quest for the fabled Marias Pass. He would determine its suitability, if it indeed existed, as a westward passage for James J. Hill's railroad.

The 36-year-old Stevens was described as wiry and athletic in build and a self-taught, tenacious New Englander with the middle name of "nerve."

Stevens came from Gardiner, Maine, and he received his education at the University of Maine at Farmington. Whatever his degree, the city of Minneapolis hired him as assistant city engineer. From there he went up the ladder, working for four railroads, and advancing from surveyor's assistant to self-taught civil engineer, and finally chief engineer of the Great Northern Railway.

With Stevens came a pack team, its driver and a saddle horse. As they progressed westward, the going got too rough for the driver (who had a drinking problem), and he refused to continue. At Badger Creek Blackfeet Agency, Stevens convinced a grumbling, reluctant Flathead Indian named Coonsah to accompany him. Coonsah was wanted for murder on the Flathead Reservation and had sought sanctuary with the Blackfeet.

Soon they were slowly struggling up the eastern slope of the Rocky Mountains on Two Medicine Creek, a tributary of the Marias River, near the present-day eastern entrance to Glacier National Park. They had made snowshoes from materials found at the agency, for easier movement through the two- to four-foot-deep snow. Once they were enveloped by the cold, forbidding mountain peaks, Coonsah decided he would go no further because of the bad spirits in the pass.

Camp was made and Stevens stopped only long enough to pull off his heaviest clothing, then pressed on.

Previously, Stevens had set up his survey instruments on the plain and had taken a bearing on the elusive pass. The broad gap was supposedly visible from quite a distance, but he already had failed to find it twice.

Stevens finally came to the source of the stream. Had he found the "real" Marias Pass Summit? (Manitoba Road engineer W.D. Barclay had stopped short two years previous at a false summit.) Trembling with excitement, Stevens checked his barometer, which told him that he was barely 5,000 feet above sea level. To make sure, he continued west until he discovered another stream (later named Bear Creek) flowing west in the Pacific watershed. He had found the pass.

But now, the cold and weary Stevens had to think of survival in forty-below-zero weather. He wrote:

> The short days of winter made a rapid move necessary and after a terrifically hard and exhausting struggle, I managed to get back to the summit where I remained all night.
>
> It was almost impossible to build and keep a fire going, so I tramped a track about 100 yards in length and walked back and forth until enough daylight broke to make it safe to travel.
>
> One advantage of the extreme cold was that the mosquitoes didn't bother me.

Returning to the camp, he found the sleeping Coonsah half frozen, but alive. Apparently the campfire had gone out during the night. Together they struggled down the remainder of the 1,500-foot pass to the safety of the Indian agency. Stevens elected to travel by stagecoach, and dismissed the pack train driver.

When Hill and his investors received word of the discovery,

via the telegraph office at Fort Assinniboine, they were greatly relieved, and began at once to plan how to traverse the pass by rail next spring. Not everyone was happy, however; the dream of Paris Gibson to have the railroad go west from Great Falls was dashed.

The discovery gave Hill a railroad route to the coast that was 100 miles shorter than the other lines, and would save thousands of dollars. It also resulted in less curvature, lighter, easier grades and a virtual straight line across the Continental Divide. It was the lowest railway pass on the Divide, in the United States and north of New Mexico.

In 1893, Stevens found and surveyed the final passage—to be named Stevens Pass—through the Cascade Mountains to the Puget Sound at Everett, Washington. A 2.5-mile-long tunnel would be cut through here, replacing the original series of switchbacks.

That earlier switchback roadbed through the mountains had been called a modern engineering model. The tunnel was called "Hill's Folly," because no one thought that such a tunnel could be built 5,000 feet below the peak of the mountains—no one except Hill and his engineers. The three-year project of dynamiting and digging through solid granite employed as many as 1,565 men at one time.

The Great Falls *Daily Tribune* of December 23, 1900, proclaimed "Hill's Folley Has Become Hill's Greatest Triumph."

An earlier engineering triumph for Stevens had been Two Medicine Bridge, located just east of the summit of Marias Pass. The 214-foot-high wooden trestle was more than twice as long as it was high. It survived until 1900, when a steel bridge was constructed. The old bridge had had to be closed in windy weather because it noticeably swayed, its timbers creaking and groaning.

Stevens later became chief engineer of the Panama Canal; and, in 1917, headed a group of American experts sent to operate the Trans-Siberian and Chinese railways. He then headed an eastern American railroad and finally opened his own engineering firm.

Perhaps the highlight of Stevens' life was July 21, 1926, when a ceremony was held at the Marias Summit on the southern border of Glacier Park. Here the Upper Missouri Historical Expedition unveiled a bronze statue—about 12 feet high—of John Stevens, in recognition of his discovery of Marias Pass on December 11, 1889. He joked at the ceremony that "he felt a little like a corpse since few men have statues unveiled while they are still living…" (The expedition, sent west from St. Paul, was sponsored by the Great Northern Railway, and the historical societies of Minnesota, North Dakota and Montana.)

This should conclude the story: the legendary lost pass had been found. However, Marias Pass had long been known, and traveled, by Indians and trappers alike.

Early records have mentioned the use of Marias Pass by Kootenai, Flathead and Shoshone Indians since the 1700s. These people crossed Marias Pass to hunt buffalo on the broad plains of north-central Montana. Contrary to legend, the Lewis and Clark Expedition did not attempt to locate the pass. Lewis explored Two Medicine Creek in a futile attempt (because of cloudy weather) to determine the longitude and latitude of its headwaters. He had hoped to extend the Louisiana Purchase into rich fur lands of southern Canada.

Marias Pass became of national interest when Congress appropriated $150,000 to explore and survey railroad routes between the Mississippi River and the Pacific Ocean in 1853. Army engineer Isaac Stevens became the leader of the northernmost expedition to explore and survey a railroad route from the headwaters of the Mississippi River to Puget Sound. The "lost" pass came to Steven's attention when he examined records of western explorers including Lewis and Clark.

Isaac Stevens also was appointed governor of Washington Territory, and Indian commissioner. In the latter role, he received personal confirmation of the pass's existence from Piegan Chief Little Dog. The Piegan chief told him "that while the pass was little used and much overgrown with brush, it was visible and with some labor a pack train could be taken through it." The pass had been virtually abandoned by western tribes because of ambushes by the Blackfeet.

Stevens sent civil engineer A.W. Tinkham and a party, which included legendary Hugh Monroe as guide, from their western base to find the pass.

The Tinkham party found an eastward-flowing river to follow north of Flathead Lake that eventually branched into two tributaries. They chose the northeast stream—called Nyack Creek—and struggled up a deep valley. At its summit, the previous winter's snow was unmelted. The 7,600-foot-high gorge had a path only wide enough for a single horse and rider. This false Marias Pass—or Cut Bank Pass as it is called—was unfit for a railroad.

It is difficult to believe that experienced guides and trappers, such as Hugh Monroe and Louis Dauphin, could not have located the pass—if they had wanted to. Both knew the region well. Perhaps they saw the discovery as a threat to the Blackfeet way of life and deliberately took the wrong trail. Monroe, after all, lived with the Blackfeet and had married into the tribe.

Another railroad survey party under James Doty left Fort Benton for one last attempt to find it. This party also was accompanied by Hugh Monroe. Doty's party explored the tributaries of the Marias River, but found nothing. Doty concluded the pass was only a myth.

Isaac Stevens still believed that not all avenues of approach had been explored. He had been handicapped by not enough men or money. This optimism would give James J. Hill hope as to its existence.

Meanwhile the "lost" pass continued to be used and appeared on several maps, both civilian and military. Among these was the De Lacey map of 1865, which had been prepared for the Montana Territory government.

The passage "officially" was discovered in November 1888 by Duncan McDonald. McDonald had spent the last two years exploring for mining properties and had spoken of the pass's existence to a Deer Lodge newspaper. He believed it would make a fine route for Hill's railroad. McDonald was considered an expert on the area, as was his father, Angus. Angus McDonald had headed the last of Hudson Bay Company's fur trading posts at Fort Connah in the Flathead Valley.

The same year, Major M.D. Baldwin, former Blackfeet Indian agent, left Great Falls to explore the region between Flathead Lake, the Marias Summit and the south fork of the Marias—called Two Medicine Creek. On his return, he told the *Great Falls Tribune* that "it is the easiest and most available pass in the Rocky Mountains for a railroad." According to the newspaper report, Baldwin was going to contact Hill and tell him of his findings.

While the evidence presented would not seem to substantiate John Stevens' discovery as original, the railroad contended otherwise. They argued that there were many gateways through the mountains and that Stevens had found the right one.

Railway Age Magazine said of Stevens' feat: "Probably the most spectacular individual achievement of his career was the discovery of Marias Pass."

Whatever the facts, history has awarded John Stevens the glory of the discovery, along with honoring his great engineering feats.

ANOTHER CONSEQUENCE of Stevens' discovery was the creation of Glacier National Park. The main Great Northern Railway route passed through and promoted country almost unequaled in scenic beauty, which became the southern edge of Glacier National Park. These mountains and forests were called "some of the greatest in the country." The park's creation on May 11, 1910, was one of the Gifford Pinchot's last acts as the first chief of the Forestry Service. Along with former president Theodore Roosevelt, Pinchot began the major program of national conservation and preservation of public lands.

Lambert & Its Lady Rodeo Rider
Edna Kronkright, 1899-1977

HAVRE, FOR A TIME, had one of the finest rodeos in Montana, if not in the West. However, the Great Northern Stampede ceased when its creator, "Long" George Francis, died in a winter automobile accident, and a long drought began to take its toll on the local economy. Finally, Hill County built a new racetrack and fairgrounds in 1929, located on the west end of town on the former ranch property of Havre area vice king, Christopher "Shorty" Young.

To the new rodeo came Edna Ethel Kronkright—originally from Lambert, Montana—with her string of horses. A High Line newspaper called her "one of the best known riders and breeders in the state, with some rather swift entries," and also said she was "one of the outstanding riders in the West."

Kronkright disappeared from the racing game in the fall of 1933, when she retired and married for the second time. She had begun her career at the age of fourteen, riding for future first husband, Wilfred "Curley" Bell.

The beginnings of her career coincided with the economic rise of Lambert and all the small ranching-farming communities in the newly created Richland County, broken off from Dawson County in 1914.

If the 1939 researcher for the WPA *Montana Guide Book* had made a right turn from Sidney, the county seat of Richland County, instead of following the main road and Yellowstone River south to Glendive, he or she would have found themselves on a gravel road (Montana Highway 23) that climbed some 200 feet paralleling Fox Creek onto the benchland of the northern High Plains. The 29-mile trip through the rolling grasslands led to the community of Lambert. By then, river-irrigated sugar beet fields had been abandoned in favor of what the semi-arid country was meant for: growing grains and raising cattle. Although smaller today, Lambert still stands on the west edge of alkali-laden Fox Lake. With the railroad tracks now gone, the wind blows the lake waters to the edge of town.

THIS AREA CAME to life in about 1910 when the rains returned, the Homestead Act increased land claims by a second 160 acres, and the prove-up period was shortened. Its neighbor town to the west on Redwater Creek, Enid, also boomed with settlers, and new residents whispered of a coming two-story railroad depot, two-story school, and "...all kinds of shops and stores."

The Great Northern Railway advertised the country in countless train-car exhibits, handbills, and newspaper articles in the U.S. and abroad. Lambert soon boasted a newspaper in the large business district, along with two banks, a movie theater and even an opera house.

To this flourishing area came Orrel (O.H.) and Nettie Kronkright from Nebraska. In 1895, they and his parents located at Hathaway, between Forsyth and Miles City on the Yellowstone River. Orrel worked for several of the large cattle and sheep companies before moving to the soon-to-be Richland County in 1909, operating a hotel and livery stable business at Newlon, south of Sidney. The family, and his now-widowed mother, moved to the Fox Lake area in 1913, a year before the Great Northern Railway developed a town site called Lambert and built its spur line from Sidney.

Kronkright built a house and barn, and then began farming on his 320-acre homestead. He added a real estate and insurance business, and drove one of the first automobiles in the area. Politically, he went from the local school board to a two-year term as a county commissioner. By 1920, his oldest daughters Leona and

Mabel were married, two sons lived at Belton, Montana, and four daughters were still at home.

He was a favorite topic of the local *Promoter* newspaper, along with how well the town was growing, and how the railroad was shipping large numbers of cattle and many tons of wheat at Sidney.

Edna first gained notice in the paper in 1913 with a simple paragraph, "Wilfred Bell is training a string of his horses to be used in the relay race at the Dawson County (Glendive) Fair. Miss Edna Kronkright will ride them." We don't know how or where she met Bell, but possibly her love of horses led to her first watching him train them, and then helping out, and learning more riding skills in the process.

Bell's family first came to Montana from "French Canada," and resided in the Frenchtown area in the Clark Fork River valley, founded in 1864.

Glendive, seat of Dawson County, began with the arrival of the Northern Pacific Railroad, and a town of 5,000 developed with the established railroad shops/division offices, and shipping center for the ranchers, dry farming and irrigated sugar beet industry. Thus, Glendive became the largest town in east-central Montana, and of course offered the best fair and rodeo.

This first rodeo went well for Bell and Kronkright. Bell's horse, "Dixie," won the five-eights mile race, but no mention was made of its rider. Next came the motorcycle race with Excelsiors against Indian-brand bikes. Stunt flying, parachute jumps and auto races were also popular. Edna's career began in the ladies' relay race, in which three horses were usually ridden at least a half-mile each, riders changing horses at each stop. Her competitors were three local women and a Mrs. Julia Lynch of Miles City—Montana's "Cowboy Capital," located seventy-eight miles to the southwest on the Yellowstone River. Edna bested Lynch the first day by only a few feet, with Mrs. C. Johnson third and Mrs. Blanche Roberts trailing.

Before the second race, Mrs. Lynch reported that one of her

horses had gone lame, and she wanted to substitute KC, which had won the five-eights-mile dash. The track veterinarian said the original horse was okay to run, but Lynch withdrew anyway. This should have left Edna a clear path to victory, except Johnson won the second heat, while Lynch continued her winning ways on KC in the five-eights mile running race. The third heat of the relay race saw another hot contest, with Edna doing a better job of changing horses, in spite of having trouble keeping one horse on the track when it wanted to run back into the paddock area. But "the little miss from Fox Lake" made up the distance and won by half a second; this giving her a three day running time of 19 minutes, 1.5 seconds. Interestingly, the bronc riders received no newspaper coverage.

This concluded Edna's brief 1913 test-run racing season, but she and Wilfred came back the following summer with an expanded rodeo agenda.

The folks at Lambert decided the growing, prosperous town should have its own rodeo. In fact, they were even talking about incorporating the community. The Lambert rodeo reportedly attracted about two thousand people, about four times the town's population. Edna and Wilfred dominated the racing action, including W.B.'s winning the foot race, and they took home about $35.00, a month's cowboy wage.

The couple again entered the Glendive–Dawson County Fair Races. He won the one-half mile cowpony race and cowboy relay race, while she won the ladies' relay race—called the fair's most exciting event—as she dueled with Mrs. Cage Johnston. Also important to her, though, was besting her last year's time by about twenty-two seconds. She also went north of Sidney to ride at the Fairview Rodeo with her own string of horses.

In 1915, the nearby town of Poplar was briefly the county seat of Roosevelt County, and Edna Kronkright and Wilfred Bell participated in their rodeo. The pair began appearing on the social page of the *Promoter* as a couple, besides continuing to increase their rodeo activities. They continued to dominate the Lambert rodeo with Bell even winning the bucking-horse contest, and continuing his reign as the foot race champion. Edna's sister, Mabel, challenged her in the quarter-mile ladies' pony race, only to finish second. No times were given. Apparently only Wilfred entered the quarter-mile men's pony race, and Edna entered to make it a contest.

The Lambert fair grew in stature, bringing in a distinguished public speaker and the brass band from the county seat at Sidney, but the attendance was down because of that year's inclement weather. In between showers, the local baseball team played the neighboring team at Enid. Enid also had a rodeo that helped to make the Bells a little richer.

In the beginning of 1916 the *Promoter* gushed with the announcement that a double wedding had taken place at Fairview. Edna married Wilfred, and her brother, George Kronkright, united with Nellie Crawford of Three Buttes, Richland County. The editor praised Bell as having a "sterling character and [being] the most expert horseman of eastern Montana" and Edna as "a young woman of high attainments and pleasing personality with a wide circle of friends." A reception and dance were held for them at the opera house.

Glendive, feeling its prosperity and growth, held two rodeos in 1916: a Fourth of July town "stampede," and the other the usual rodeo events at the fall Dawson County Fair. Edna was the overall winner in the cowgirls' relay race, although her sister Mabel—riding as Mrs. Charles Darling—edged her out on the second day. Edna came in second in the cowgirls' half-mile dash, losing to Mrs. Cage Johnson, while Wilfred bested Cage Johnson in the Men's Relay Race.

The city and its American Legion post spent a good amount of money on prizes, and attracted such champion riders as Tex Harris, Pinky Gist, Powder Lee, and the "Panama Kid." In the fall Dawson County Fair rodeo, Edna again battled Mrs. Cage Johnson in the ladies' relay race, winning the event. Sister Mabel finished third.

However, this wasn't the big event for Edna in 1916. She decided to compete against the best performers in the $2,000 relay race for "the Championship of the World" at the Montana State Fair in Helena. The eight-mile, three-day event featured a horse change every half-mile. The top performers in the event were Nellie Parsons from Polson, Montana, and Ruth Gordon of Toppenish, Washington. Established rodeo star Fanny Sperry Steele of Helena did not participate; she and her husband were performing in Billings businessman C.L. Harris's "Passing of the West" show. Afterwards they traveled east to rodeos in New York, Chicago, Milwaukee, and Kansas City.

Edna did not win, place or show, although she was mentioned as an entrant. Parsons and Parton were perennial competitors, with each holding wins against the other. The crowd saw the expected duel between them, with the third-place rider coming in about thirty-five seconds behind the two. Edna would have been in fourth place.

This obviously would be a good training experience once she got over the humiliation, and it may have been the reason she started buying thoroughbreds from around the country instead of raising them.

Edna resumed her Montana, South Dakota and Nebraska circuit (and probably traveled to other locations, including in Canada), adding the Wolf Point Rodeo when that town became the permanent county seat of Roosevelt County. Both she and Wilfred continued their winning ways, although Edna lost the 1917 ladies' relay race in Glendive, by one second, to Mrs. Leo Rodman. The ladies' relay race continued to be the focus of interest for fans, said the writer in the *Glendive Review*. The Billings–Yellowstone County Midland Empire event was next on their list to conquer. Billings was the third-largest city in Montana, and the first in eastern Montana, at about 16,000 souls. That rodeo was a stop for top national performers. The Lambert *Promoter* described the Bells as winners there in 1918-1919, giving no details.

It was rare for newspapers to praise women riders, but the

Glendive Review called her "the racing jockey/relay rider" and "a clever rider who dominated in eastern Montana."

While Edna's career continued its upward arc, the country around her began its downward spiral. The rains that had turned eastern Montana into a farmer's oasis began to diminish. In some sections of the state, little or no rain fell. There were some wet years, but the climate stayed mostly dry until the 1940s. Some ranchers survived the 1920s, but lost their holdings in the 1930s. Farmers lost their lands to the bank, but the mortgages were worthless paper and several banks went under also. Making it worse, when World War I ended in 1919, government crop price-supports ceased.

Next came national prohibition. The rum runners going back and forth across the border to wet Canada stopped at isolated towns like Lambert to rob local merchants, who were barely hanging on. By 1925, the business district of Lambert counted several vacant buildings, and apparent arson fires continued.

Town rodeos all but disappeared, and county fair/rodeos continued, but on a spottier schedule. The Kronkright family, among others, headed for greener pastures, leaving the community that once competed with Sidney to be county seat. After a short sojourn in Columbia Falls, Montana, and Priest River, Idaho, the Kronkright parents settled in Clancy, south of the capital at Helena.

Wilfred Bell broke his arm in a 1926 rodeo, and worked as a veterinarian's assistant in Sidney until it mended. Meanwhile, Edna started spending winters with her parents and other sisters.

One rodeo that didn't falter was the Wolf Point Stampede, where some of the best races occurred. The town takes pride in its continuous existence. Edna became a special friend of the American Legion manager, Ray Mitchell. Mitchell had a ranch just out of town, and Edna, at about thirty, moved in with him in the late 1920s, just after his wife, Lucy, died. Mitchell had lived in the Wolf Point area since about 1922, moving there from Miles City after participating in World War I. He produced the rodeo and operated a livery barn with the Clark brothers. Mitchell lost his rodeo manager job when the local Commercial Club took over the rodeo from the American Legion.

After separating from Wilfred, Edna started using the Mitchell name at times, or letting a rodeo still list her as Edna or Mrs. Wilfred Bell, or listing her horses as Mitchell's. Edna had been living in Sidney while Bell had moved to Cody, Wyoming, working summers at a dude ranch. They began the rodeo circuit together, but Mitchell, at about forty, had apparently tired of the sport, and moved back to Miles City with Edna, and started working at the Fort Keogh Agricultural Experiment Station.

He drowned in the nearby Yellowstone River in 1934. His family's obituary made it definite that Mitchell didn't marry twice.

Also in the 1920s, Edna became friends with former Lambert residents Roy and Jesse France. The trio followed the rodeo circuit together, even helping each other in riding. The two women really put on a show against each other in the relay races. When Havre rejoined the rodeo circuit after an eight-year hiatus in 1929, it fitted into the schedule between the Chinook and Glasgow rodeos. The smaller rodeos drew fewer competitors, so Edna got to ride in the men's events, such as the roman (two-horse) standing race.

In the 1930 Chinook rodeo, Edna rode against the competitive Ranger family that included both dad Mose and daughter Doris. She defeated Mose and local favorite Steve Adams Jr. in the roman race. She also won the seven-eights-mile race, but lost to Doris in the ladies' relay race. An ongoing competition between them continued at Havre and Glasgow. At some rodeos, when she wasn't allowed to race with the men, she rode by herself and compared their times, which usually were higher.

But by 1931, Edna may have become discouraged with racing because of the emotional and financial drain of having lost three horses: one at the Richland County Fair, another at Deadwood, North Dakota, and one of her finest horses, Marble Arch, at the Culbertson racetrack. She still continued trips to see her family in the off season.

The town of Lambert was also having its problems after another major fire struck, causing $50,000 in damage. The area had received a major rainfall in 1928, which produced the best wheat crop since 1916, but the drought returned the following year.

Sometime in this period she met Ray Mavity, a national rodeo star. The Mavity family had lived northwest of Lambert on Redwater Creek. Edna and Ray married in August of 1933 at Forsyth, Montana. In him, she finally met a rodeo man who was younger. In fact, Edna was five years older than he was. Ray's winning rodeo career had begun in his late teens.

Edna quit the rodeo circuit, but kept her horses—perhaps boarding them with her folks at Clancy. Mavity had a gold mine somewhere in the Clancy-Basin area, and he operated a saw mill near Ovando, Montana. With Ray, she traveled to all the major rodeos in the United States, and saw the likes of New York, Boston and Chicago. Mavity helped establish the Rodeo Cowboy Association, and the Cowboys' Turtle Association to initiate some regulation for protecting competitors from fraud, and develop a uniform national ranking system.

Ray's star continued to rise when, in 1935, he was named the National Champion Bronc Rider, and in 1939 the Champion Steer Decorator (in the event that had replaced steer wrestling). Because of his rodeo stature, Edna got to join him in the Butte grand entry parade as they rode palominos with two of the best national women riders, Alice and Marjorie Greenough of Red Lodge, Montana. Mavity had won the bronc riding contest the year before and the Livingston and Lewistown, Montana, rodeos that year. The Butte newspaper called Mavity the "toughest hombre" and "wildest bronc buster in the game today." It also bragged of their rodeo's major status following those at Calgary, Alberta; Nampa, Idaho; and Salt Lake City.

The Mavitys retired from the rodeo world, perhaps around 1945, after her mother's death. They moved to Anchorage, in the shadow of the Chugach Mountains at the head of Cook Inlet,

Gulf of Alaska. The area boomed in the 1940s and 1950s with the development of air, seaport and land military bases. Pearl Kronkright-Gingerich also lived there, working for the State of Alaska and then the Richfield Oil Company.

Ray apparently worked as a heavy equipment operator. Edna operated a café in town.

They experienced the horror of a lifetime in 1964, when a major earthquake struck, in which Anchorage was heavily damaged and, in places, the earth sank. The damage was in the billions of dollars, and more than one hundred people lost their lives.

The Mavitys returned to Montana in 1970, and settled in the Bitterroot River Valley at Stevensville. Ray died about four years later at Basin, still mining for gold. He is buried in the Carlton cemetery in Florence, near Stevensville. Edna died in July of 1977 at Saint Patrick's Hospital in Missoula. She had been residing with sister Pearl Gingerich, first in Stevensville and then in the Columbia Falls area. She was buried next to Ray. Her obituary stated that she became a relay and thoroughbred racehorse rider at the age of eleven (actually fourteen).

Edna had been one of the most consistent rodeo winners in eastern Montana, over a twenty-year period on the smaller rodeo and fair circuit, yet when she did ride against "better" riders, she did well (except the early Helena episode). Unfortunately, she and her family, who were a major part of early-day Lambert, have been forgotten, not even mentioned in the Lambert museum.

While the Kronkright family apparently has died out in name, the town of Lambert has not. It survived major fires and the loss of the railroad. The town on Montana Highway 200 is now home to 135 people, still has a business section, two churches and a lovely park. Stop in sometime and visit at the senior citizen center and the museum. They have good stories, if—sadly—none about Edna, Wilfred, Roy or Ray.

One wonders if any Kronkright descendants return to Lambert for its annual July Fourth community event, or whether one relative somewhere has a scrapbook of Edna, her family and beloved horses: the likes of Silver Lady, Red Weed, I Know, Marble Arch, Carlos Enrique…

Blood on the Trail

Shootout in Little Box Elder Creek Canyon, 1887-1888

THE MOST PROMINENT physical feature in north central Montana is the Bear's Paw Mountains. From these peaks flow several creeks, either south to the Missouri River or north to the Milk River. One of these tributaries of the Milk is called Little Box Elder Creek, flowing across the former town site of Toledo and under U.S. Highway #2 and the Burlington Northern Railway tracks, seven miles east of Havre, the regional hub.

A historic site in Havre is the first public cemetery—called Mount Hope—on a windswept hilltop just south of the Milk River Valley. In the section with unmarked graves, the body of a Métis (French-Indian) man, known only as "Bluebird," is believed to be buried. This once large-framed, tall figure had served as a military scout at nearby Fort Assinniboine during the Indian conflicts in eastern Montana. As possibly once a buffalo hunter in the eastern Montana Territory himself, he would have been quite familiar with the haunts of other mixed-blood Indian people of Plains Cree and Chippewa ancestry. This would have included their primary home at Juneau's Fort on Frenchman's Creek, where the military watched for illegal trade of alcohol, gun and ammunition to Indian bands.

Bluebird had been a scout at the large and imposing military fort until November 1887, when he was reportedly either discharged for thievery, or left the area still wanted for his crimes. He made the center of his new illegal activities near the combination trading post and Gros Ventre–Upper Assiniboine Indian agency at Fort Belknap, a complex south of present-day town of Chinook and adjacent to the Milk River.

The outlaw apparently stole by day, concealed the goods in his most-likely appropriated military tent, and rustled Fort Belknap agency horses with the ID brand from their fenced pastures by night. When he was finally spotted, an unknown number of reservation residents—perhaps Indian police—took up the chase.

A running gun battle ensued, with the rustler at a probable disadvantage with his U.S. Army Springfield single-shot carbine—against lever-action rifles. Near present Chinook, "Bluebird" was forced to abandon the horses and try to save himself. (This may have been because he was wounded.) He fled west along the frozen Milk River for several miles, turning south across the recently laid railroad tracks of the Great Northern, through an elevated flat that later held the short-lived town site of Toledo, and entered the valley of Little Box Elder Creek. The former scout probably knew the area well because the army had had a summer encampment there; also the military trail he was following led to Fort Assinniboine, ten miles southwest. Even if the army had jailed him, he at least wouldn't be killed by his trackers, and he would have had the benefit of an army surgeon.

However, if this was his plan, "Bluebird" was apparently unable to stay in the saddle, weakened by his wound. By then, too, his horse must have been spent. Hence, he crossed the snow-covered quarter-mile wide-valley floor to where numerous outcroppings of rock were located. He may have followed the Spring Coulee that split off east from the main valley. Bluebird took refuge behind a large rock and the adjacent valley wall. He took the saddle off his pinto horse, trying to unsuccessfully shoo the animal away. He placed his tent overhead, securing it with rocks, and on both sides, he piled rocks and branches. Lastly, with adequate cover and concealment, he placed his rifle in an opening and awaited his fate.

For two days he fought a gun battle with his pursuers, killing four, before he took a rifle round in the head. The remainder of his trackers left without disturbing the defensive site, perhaps showing respect for Bluebird's fighting abilities.

The following year, Fort Belknap Indian Reservation was reduced in size, and the former battleground became part of the Auld family ranch. An unidentified ranch employee said he rode through that area on a regular basis, but saw only the horse, which he tried unsuccessfully to drive away.

Finally, in 1901, John Lynch discovered a skeleton while hunting coyotes. He felt no need to report it to the county authorities. The following year a Chouteau County Coroner's Jury was organized in Havre to view the now well-known site, with Lynch guiding them to it.

They found that the site had deteriorated from the effects of time and wild animals. They found the skeletal remains of Bluebird in his improvised fortress and his faithful horse's skeleton not far away. His body showed the effects of bullets that had splintered two ribs and put a hole through one side of his skull. Further examination further showed he had suffered a broken right shoulder and arm, possibly during a past buffalo hunt. Both his tent and army coat showed evidence of his bleeding wound. Near him was his saddle, now leather-less, chewed by coyotes, and twenty-spent spent fifty-caliber cartridges. The blue coat was the only article of clothing that retained its color and bulk, although only two brass buttons remained.

The remainder of items included other clothing, bedding and metal saddle remnants, one partially-chewed moccasin, a medicine bone necklace, a Bowie knife, a hair brush, tin cup, and other personal effects. Although its was now tattered and faded, his clothing obviously had been of good quality. Only his rifle and cap were missing.

At the time of his burial, the coroner's jury did not know any of Bluebird's story, why he died there or at whose hands. Finally local cowboy and former military scout, Louie Shambo (Chambeau), once employed at Fort Assinniboine, told what he knew of the man and what had transpired that freezing winter's day. Shambo apparently didn't know the man's French name either. Was it Bluebird because he had fled the Army? Or was his real name Azure? Could the answer lie in the records of the Turtle Mountain Reservation in North Dakota? All unknown.

Perhaps now as people drive between Chinook and Havre, near the Blaine County–Hill County line, their journey will be a little more meaningful as they pass near the site of the mystery man who perished there, along with brave men from Fort Belknap—and a faithful horse.

Glasgow, 1894

HAVRE MAY HAVE HAD a violent history, at least in the red light district, however the town couldn't claim to have had a "real west" experience of a man-to-man, face-to-face gunfight, as could the cowboy town of Glasgow.

In the Glasgow–Valley County area spread some of the largest cattle ranches in Montana, including the N Bar N Ranch of the Neidringhaus Brothers of St. Louis. Employment rolls of the N Bar N had listed such gunmen as Harry Longabaugh ("Sundance Kid"), Armour Broome, Jack Teal, "Long" Henry Thompson, "Dutch" Henry Ieuch, Plaz Price, Tom Dunn, and George Dunnell.

These large cattle companies ended in northern Montana after the winter of 1906-1907 but, until then, Glasgow claimed the title as the cowboy capital of the Milk River Country—besides boasting the #45 railroad siding west of Minot, North Dakota, on the Great Northern Railway.

One of the Wyoming cowboys who drifted into Glasgow after the Johnson County War (among Wyoming cattlemen, when small-spread ranchers tried to fight off the controlling large-spread owners) was Martin Allison Tisdale, calling himself "Al Allison" in Montana. Tisdale appeared on the Wyoming Stock Growers Association (WSGA) "wanted" list for rustling in Johnson County, northern Wyoming. Supposedly Tisdale had a $2,500 reward on his head.

When the independent Northern Wyoming Farmers and Association formed at the town of Buffalo in 1892, the statewide WSGA at Cheyenne—well connected with state government—lumped all the new group's members into the outlaw category. Their other "outlaws" included cowboys who had started their spreads by mavericking, or claiming unbranded calves off the open range.

In Buffalo, however, the local court supported the Northern Wyoming group, to the WSGA's frustration. The latter resorted to war, with hired guns on its side. And it blackballed cowboys who had worked for ranchers in the independent Northern association.

WSGA forces mounted an aborted invasion of Johnson County in 1892, with a "kill list" of seventy ranchers, Buffalo townspeople, and city-county officials.

The plan failed when the fifty-man party detoured to the KC ranch, fifty miles south of Buffalo, where Nate Champion and Nick Ray could be found. WSGA considered Champion a leader of the "rustlers and grangers," and Ray a Northern member. However, Champion put up such an extended fight, before he was killed, that word reached Buffalo and an opposing force was formed. The invaders reached safe haven at the TA ranch, fourteen miles south of Buffalo, where they were surrounded. Only by the arrival of soldiers from nearby Fort McKinney saved the WSGA men; then they removed themselves from Johnson County's jurisdiction. The WSGA reportedly singled out Tisdale as one of the resistance leaders.

Texans Martin Allison Tisdale, along with his older brother John A., were partners in the "Hat Outfit," a major competitor of the Cheyenne cattle barons. Their leader was a Oscar "Jack" Flagg, who was also given credit for being the brains of the "outlaws." WSGA called his ranch the most notorious rustling outfit in Wyoming; that is, after they had illegally blackballed its cowboys.

Martin's brother John, a college graduate, brought his family to Wyoming after managing the Northern Pacific Railroad stockyards at Mandan, North Dakota. The Tisdales came from Williamson County, Texas, of a well-respected Methodist and Masonic family. Apparently John's only sin, which caused his murder, was his association with the Hat outfit.

Martin was called the black sheep of their family, having left home at a young age to become a cowboy-rancher and possibly a rustler in New Mexico. After his brother was killed, he moved further into the sights of the WSGA when he tried to pursue local legal action against the alleged assassins, rancher Fred Hesse and former lawman Frank Canton.

Martin Tisdale left Wyoming with a party of men on his tail, who were inclined to want him dead. His faithful longtime horse, "White Man," outran them despite the pursuing party's obtaining fresh horses.

When Tisdale landed in Glasgow, he made a dangerous enemy of George Dunnell.

The background of outlaw Dunnell is more vague. We know he was raising horses and cattle by 1900, and he worked as a Valley County deputy sheriff and state stock inspector. His achievements included helping to tame the area's rustling gangs and arresting the major rustler, "Dutch" Henry, and that he had rescued a Canadian Mountie from sure death by outlaws at Culbertson. Dunnell was apparently well-liked around Glasgow, but thought to be not one to mess with.

The argument between Dunnell and Tisdale had to do with two horses that Tisdale "claimed Dunnell lost for him." Dunnell may have been working as a stock inspector at the time, and found that Tisdale didn't have title to the horses in dispute. Reportedly they also had clashed earlier.

Their Glasgow face-off took place at about 11 P.M. in an alley off First Street, between McMillan's Saloon and the Waldo House, where Tisdale was staying. A heated argument ended with Tisdale saying he would get his revolver to finish deciding who was telling the truth. Dunnell replied he would kill Tisdale if he brought back his gun. Tisdale ignored the threat, but went to his room for his pistol. He walked back down the corridor, holding his revolver up to the light to make sure it was fully loaded (others must have accompanied him). At the hotel entrance, he calmly exchanged greetings with Undersheriff Caldwell.

Tisdale approached the alley with his hand on the butt of his weapon, which was fully tucked in his pants. He was silhouetted by the McMillan saloon lights, while Dunnell stood in the shadows of McMillan's entrance, his revolver out. Dunnell ordered Tisdale to stop, and not to reach for his gun, or he would shoot. Tisdale answered: "What's the matter with you?" and kept walking toward Dunnell, turning to the side to lessen himself as a target.

Their two guns exploded about the same time—Tisdale's perhaps slightly sooner, according to witnesses. Tisdale fired from the hip, and his three shots went wild through the saloon windows. Dunnell fired four times, striking Tisdale in the right hand, tearing off part of the gun butt, and hitting Tisdale's upper left arm and right breast. Tisdale fell backward on the saloon porch, attempting to fire again before he died.

Dunnell handed his weapon over to the undersheriff. Tisdale's body was laid out in the Waldo House office, and an impromptu

In a Glasgow cowboy grouping, George Dunnell is center, in dark hat. VALLEY COUNTY HISTORICAL SOCIETY, GLASGOW, MT

coroner's inquest convened. There could be only one conclusion: Tisdale died from a bullet fired by George Dunnell.

A preliminary hearing in justice court followed the next day. The judge ruled justifiable homicide since "the murdered man was a hard case and regarded life lightly.",The newspaper stated that Tisdale had gone bad after his brother's death in the Johnson County War, "and finally lost the respect of everyone." Yet in addition, "he was generous, kind and indulgent [when sober], and would go to any trouble to serve [others]."

The day before Tisdale died, he told his friends he wasn't destined to live long because he had consumption. His big worry was the future of his old, faithful horse, White Man. He hoped to find a caring owner who wouldn't abuse him. Rancher "Doc" Smith volunteered to give the steed an easy life in his old age.

Most wanted men then in northern Montana were never discovered as long they stayed out of trouble and the spotlight. Obviously Tisdale didn't care, not one whit.

Havre, 1902-1905

BESIDES THE INDIAN TRIBES, the military officials at Fort Assinniboine had to deal with men who traded in illegal alcohol, opium, prostitution and sex trafficking, arms and ammunition, plus transporting stolen horses, mules, cattle and sheep across to either side of the international border. These animals were stolen in the region of the Teton, Marias, Musselshell and Judith river basins of north and central Montana.

The criminals fed on the pay of the military, from their own settlement west of the post near Beaver Creek. The civilian settlement was legally on the military reservation because of the tenants' connection to the military or the post trader's operation. Here, in pre-Havre days, tunnels connected four cabins that supplied a soldier's desires alcohol, women and gambling. The leaders of this camp were an "Iron Mike" and "Big Sandy," apparently teamsters with the Broadwater-McCulloh post traders and transportation company. These men were eventually arrested and the camp broken up by Provost Sergeant Herman Werner.

Another early vice location was the "town" of Cypress, located at the north wagon trail crossing on Big Sandy Creek, just northwest of Beaver Creek. Although the owners pushed to develop a real town, Cypress consisted of several tent saloons with gamblers and prostitutes. Nearby, on upper Beaver Creek to the east, was a "hog ranch," located north of the present-day golf course near Black Butte.

However, these sites closed when the railroad town of Havre came into being in 1890-1901, with the westward expansion of the Great Northern Railway from the Havre area to the West Coast. The railroad first came to the Bull Hook Creek bottoms in 1887, where the town began as a boxcar depot/freight station.

The Halfway House roadhouse, on Halfway Lake near the post-to-town trail, was operated by two former soldiers, Bailey and Purnell, who also operated a saloon in the red light district of Havre. The roadhouse soon eclipsed other countryside vice operations.

As Havre developed, prospering from the business of railroaders, soldiers, coal miners, freight drivers, cowboys, etc., a large, two-block-long red light district developed on the west end of First Street. Chicago transplant Christopher W. "Shorty" Young controlled most of the gambling and prostitution; the jewel of his operations was a large building complex called the Montana Hotel/Restaurant/Concert Hall that became known as simply the "Honky-Tonk." The building had attached cribs and a parlor house that formed a U opening south to the street, the railroad tracks to its north. Here the soldiers could also spend their pay, although they were subjected to local lawmen and court after the gun smoke cleared.

The month of June, 1902, was a banner season for the number of troops occupying Fort Assinniboine in north-central Montana's Milk River country. All the other forts established in the Montana Territory during the North American Indian wars, thanks to continued political pressure by U.S. Representative Charles Pray of Fort Benton, then the Hill County seat, south on the Missouri River. Pray, a former Chicago lawyer, had to fight alone, as U.S. Senators Joseph Dixon and Thomas Carter had their own hands full, saving nonessential posts in their own towns of Missoula and Helena.

In one month, the returning soldiers from the Spanish-American War in the Philippines escalated, with Assinniboine's troop numbers, from 174 to 843. The black 24th Infantry Regiment had been transferred to the fort for rest and relaxation, and they would return to action in mid-1906. Also joining them was the white 3rd Cavalry unit. The two races got along fairly well, unless liquor was involved, and there was plenty of that at the nearby roadhouse and town of Havre, although whiskey was now prohibited at the fort's saloon.

In mid-August, 1902, a number of both 3rd Cavalry and 24th Infantry soldiers decided to go AWOL, and to stay at the Honky-Tonk until they ran out of money. They left the fort after dark, slipping by the guard posts, and walked the six miles to town.

The first night, some friction developed after the drinking began, but it was stopped before becoming serious. The following night, violence did ensue. The point of contention was over the color line that divided the dance hall and tables. The two groups were initially happily dancing and drinking with the women of the house in the wee hours of a Thursday morning, while others lined up at the bar. Then an E Company private of the 24th Infantry, J.W. Traylor, decided to cross the line. Traylor indignantly pulled up a chair at white solders' table, and began "harassing" them. Reportedly the whites tried to ignore Traylor; one of Traylor's friends crossed over to convince Traylor to return to the "colored section." However, Traylor would have none of that, as his temper (and perhaps drinking) was in high gear. He was heard to say: "I'm going to start a rough house!"

Finally a white soldier, Private Edward Poag, decided to confront Traylor (they may have had words earlier), and forced him back across the line. Traylor drew his revolver and fired one round into the ceiling and another into the floor. Then, according to ten witnesses, Poag—without uttering a word—pointed his .45 Colt revolver at Traylor's stomach, and fired four times. Poag then supposedly started backing up toward the front entrance while reloading. However, he never made it, as allegedly another black soldier got behind him and opened fire.

The witnesses—including Shorty Young—pointed to Private Joe Brooks as the second shooter. Young had not seen the first shooting because he was in his second-floor office, and a burly black corporal blocked his way out. Witnesses also mentioned seeing a tall white soldier leave the building after the shooting stopped.

Poag's companions carried him down the block to Dr. J.S. Almas's office, and Traylor was taken to an adjacent house. Meanwhile a rider notified post authorities, and the men were moved to the military hospital. The other soldiers returned to the fort after the shootings, arriving before daylight. Supposedly the black soldiers secured their rifles and started back to town "to clean things up." Colonel Albert Woodson then ordered a detachment of 3rd Cavalry men out to retrieve these soldiers before they reached town. It was later officially denied that any weapons were provided, but the black soldiers were helped back to the fort.

Back at the concert hall, witnesses also claimed that yet a third black soldier had also fired his gun. Supposedly about ten shots in total had been fired; a search of Brooks, the concert hall, and the grounds produced no weapon. Brooks denied any involvement in the shootings, saying he had just arrived at the building when the white cavalry men behind tables blazing away at Traylor. Further, that his revolver was back in his quarters. He had privates Buchanan, Balding and Brockman backing him up.

The local newspaper observed that Brooks was "a good looking colored man with more than ordinary intelligence." It added he slept well in the county jail.

Private Traylor lived for about twenty hours. He had no chance for survival, with all four large rounds entering his body at close range. Poag's prognosis wasn't much better, and he later died also.

(In a side note, when their weapons were examined, supposedly they had been switched for unfired ones.)

The coroner's inquest occurred the following week. Concert hall employees still claimed that Traylor had been killed by Poag, while two other "more reliable" witnesses, E.L. Brown and C.H. Simms, claimed another white soldier had shot Traylor. These witnesses were Caucasian and apparently army sergeants. Perhaps the house witnesses were influenced by Traylor's earlier statement to manager Gene Fenton that Poag had it in for him. Confusion reined, however, and it even was said that a fourth white soldier also fired at Traylor.

Finally, the coroner's jury announced that Traylor had been killed by gunshot wounds inflicted by Poag or a Private Everett Wall—the man the two reliable witnesses claimed killed Traylor. Wall had to be returned from Fort Keogh near Miles City, from where he had been transferred in.

Brooks was arraigned by Justice Court Judge Henry Meili and bound over to district court in Fort Benton. During Brooks' trial, Private Everett Wall admitted to emptying his revolver at Traylor. Subsequently he admitted to killing Traylor, but only in self-defense, because Traylor pointed a gun at him. Wall was the tall white soldier exiting the back door after the shootings. Wall received an eight-year manslaughter conviction for killing Traylor. The case against Brooks was dismissed, and Poag exonerated. This only left the killer of Poag. Had Brooks' rounds also struck Poag or had an unidentified black soldier in the crowd killed him? Apparently no one wanted to explore the case any further.

At another time, another 24th Infantry soldier died because of alcohol, but without the gunfire. Private Bryant was found frozen to death near the railroad tracks west of town. Bryant had spent all his money on drinks, and was apparently on his way back to the fort for Thanksgiving, even though he already had been discharged. His discharge papers weren't on the body, though. It appears the concert hall had caused another casualty.

Another former soldier, now a teamster (wagon driver), had

nearly been a casualty at the Halfway House. A prostitute at the establishment had seriously cut him up, and he barely made it back to town. His friends found him in the dray company barn, and rushed him to the doctor.

The Halfway Lake roadhouse or "resort" was the scene of the most shootings, knifings and suicides among soldiers, civilian workers and prostitutes. Since it was in Chouteau County, with the county seat some seventy-eight miles away, the roadhouse developed into a wide-open operation. It is strange that the army even tolerated it, since they had placed earlier vice operations off-limits.

Only a month after the Honky-Tonk shootings had occurred, the place became a battlefield on Christmas Eve, 1902. That night, members of the 3rd Cavalry had taken over the saloon section, and they were engaged in serious drinking and song. All was going well until a Company G cavalryman, E.J. Gans, ran out of money. He insisted the bartender, A.M. Graves, give him free drinks. When Graves refused, proprietor Charles Bolan calmed Gans down, allowing him to stay if he didn't cause any further trouble. Perhaps he even gave Gans a free drink.

That truce however didn't last long, and Gans tried to climb over the bar to get more whiskey. Graves stopped him only to have Gans come around the bar to confront the bartender. Gans received a knockdown blow for his efforts. Gans retreated behind the potbelly stove and opened fire at Graves. Graves returned the fire, shooting both Gans in the stomach, and bystander Private Robinson in the hip. Gans staggered toward the door, dropping his revolver before exiting. Apparently no one tried to go after him. Only when the next customer tried to exit did he find Gans slumped by the door in a snow bank.

Some soldiers returned to the fort for the ambulance, and both soldiers were hauled to the hospital, where the hospital crew was certainly getting much practice on bullet wounds. The prognosis for Gans was grim, and Robinson—the innocent bystander—was paralyzed from the waist down.

Afterwards, Graves thought about going to Havre and giving himself up, but instead he walked outdoors for a while, apparently hoping the situation over. Perhaps his hesitation came from the fact that he was black and Gans was white. He decided to return to the roadhouse and await law enforcement's response, which wasn't long in coming. In fact, Havre Police Chief Art White (also a Hill County deputy sheriff) showed up Christmas morning.

Graves' initial story had Gans also shooting Private Robinson, but he recanted that version. After all the facts were related, defense attorney J.S. Carnal moved to have the case dismissed, since one shot was self-defense and the other accidental. However, Justice Court Judge Henry Meili ordered Graves bound over for trial in Fort Benton District Court. Perhaps Meili was influenced by and disgusted with the continued violence at the roadhouse that had flourished since the mid-1890s.

(Once in a while the stories of violence had not-so-bad endings. For instance, in 1896, the *Milk River Herald* had related the story of a fight between two prostitutes: "Goldie" Parks, "a comely yellow-skinned siren," and a Mrs. Stratton, "a fair mulatto." The latter woman shot and wounded "Goldie" because of her attention towards Mr. Stratton. Apparently, in the end all was forgiven and the women became good friends again.)

While roadhouse bartender Graves languished in the Chouteau County jail awaiting trial, more gunfire exploded in Havre's red-light district. It started when "Kid" Fredericks, a boxer in Shorty Young's stable, shot an unknown Japanese man in Shorty's Honky-Tonk. (The railroad had brought in Japanese to work laying track.) After Fredericks put the Japanese man down for an unknown reason, he left the concert hall and roamed the streets with about ten other Japanese companions.

Then, near the city jail on First Street and Third Avenue, Chinook cowboys Tom Carrigan and Alf Gilmore met Fredericks' party on the sidewalk, and neither side wanted to yield the right of way and have to walk in the street. Soon the two cowboys went after the larger group with their fists, and the Japanese returned the favor, even stabbing both men. The wounded cowboys retreated west, grabbing their guns from inside Lamey's saloon. Another cowboy, Jim Swindle, joined the first two.

The action then shifted to Bailey & Purnell's saloon, when its patrons emptied into the streets. Both sides escalated the affair and gunfire erupted. This resulted in Carrigan's receiving another wound, and in the death of one Japanese man, an individual kicked out of the saloon. Poor, out-manned police officer William Chestnut tried to stop the violence, but there were too many people for one man to handle.

The coroner's jury ruled the yet unidentified deceased died from a gunshot by an unknown assailant. Carrigan and Gilmore were expected to survive their wounds with no charges filed.

Back at the Halfway House, violence continued into 1905. An early article described the two-story building as measuring 24'x50', with a kitchen and dining room connecting to the saloon. The upstairs had eight sleeping rooms. A second, similar building also stood on the grounds.

February started at the roadhouse with a gun battle between a retired soldier, Phillip Dixon, and current soldier, Joe Allison of E Company, 24th Infantry. Their fight was over "colored courtesan" Laura Hall. The fight spiraled outside until both men had emptied their guns. Ironically, Hall was the one who was wounded. Dixon claimed that he fired in self-defense when Allison threatened "to shoot his hide so full of holes that it would not hold Missouri corn shucks." Doctor Almas again did the repair work in Havre.

The April 1905 shooting at the roadhouse was a more serious affair. Again, it was a fight between two black cavalrymen and over the favors of a prostitute. It occurred on April 2nd at 10:45 P.M. At the time a Company E soldier, Richard Hardaway, was occupying the room of Flora Ward and refusing to leave after intimate relations. The woman returned with another customer or bystander, Robert Mudd. After exchanging angry words, Ward ordered Hardaway to leave, saying Mudd would evict him for her. Finally Hardaway grabbed his straightedge razor from under the pillow and, clothing-less, charged Mudd, saying something to the affect that he was bad and intended to cut Mudd's heart out. Hardaway got Mudd in a choke hold, ready to cut his throat, when Mudd was able to reach his revolver and fire a fatal shot. Since Mudd had an excellent reputation, having served well in the Philippines, and Hardaway had a bad one—always in trouble for something—no charges were filed.

Sporadic violence continued at the roadhouse and in Havre's red light district, but the rotation of the 24th Infantry to the Philippines ended racially-based episodes. Also, the number of troops declined until the fort was closed in 1911.

Before that date, Representative Charles Pray had continued to press for more troops, but Secretary of War William H. Taft said there were none during his 1904-1909 term, since the Army was 20,000 men short following the Spanish-American War. Pray replied to Secretary Taft and General Bell that "you have given Senator Dixon a post [Fort Missoula] and Senator Carter a post [Fort Harrison at Helena] and now you are trying to hand me a post hole. I don't want a post hole." In addition, that Pray would not acknowledge defeat until every effort was exhausted.

Pray lost the public battle, but won a personal one. He was appointed as a federal judge in Great Falls.

Havre gained, because closing Fort Assinniboine brought hordes of homesteaders to reside on the former military lands.

As, they say: "All's well that ends well."

HAVRE SUFFERED a major fire in January of 1904, which destroyed several downtown blocks. The army had to be brought in to prevent redlight-district toughs from looting piles of rescued merchandise stacked in the streets. Although the town was now the largest in Chouteau County, at about 4,000 people, surpassing the county seat of Fort Benton, it was still struggling to provide a decent sewer and water system, along with adequate police and fire departments. And, too, James J. Hill was still threatening to pull his Great Northern Railway (GNR) operation out of Havre, especially since he had taken his board of directors on a tour of west 1st Street; they saw violence everywhere.

The May 1904 installation of a reform mayor, Louis "Shorty" Newman, and initiation of his anti-vice campaign with a larger police force, came too late to save the life of city police officer Fred Stevens.

While on routine early morning patrol, the solitary policeman spotted a suspicious individual in the train yard. Stevens approached the man, noticing he matched the description of an escapee, "John Smith," from the Kalispell, Montana city jail. In a foot race among the boxcars, Stevens lost his prey. Soon after, he spotted the suspect attempting to hop a freight train, but failed to nab him. Smith instead hitched a ride on a handcar, with a railroad section crew. They were headed west to nearby Pacific Junction, where the southern line broke off to Great Falls, Helena and Butte.

Stevens caught up by horseback, and arrested the suspect where he had dropped off. Stevens started back the some four miles to Havre with the suspect walking in front. Suddenly, with the town in sight, the suspect stepped to the side of the trail and pulled out a secreted .44 revolver he had stolen from Frank Chestnut's Saloon on Havre's 3rd Avenue. Smith opened fire, first striking the horse's neck and hitting Stevens in the stomach. Stevens returned the fire, and the suspect fell to the ground after firing his last shot. The wounded Stevens and his nearly disabled horse somehow made it to town, with the policeman falling from his saddle at the doorstep of his shared residence, owned by his half-brother, hardware-store owner Henry Gross. The family carried Stevens to his bed, calling for a doctor on the new telephone system.

George Hall, state stock inspector and temporary policeman, organized and led the first posse, which included resident Chouteau County Deputy Sheriff Blevens and Chief of Police George Bickle. Arriving at the shooting scene, they found that the wanted man had fled—apparently not as wounded as Stevens had thought. On the former battleground was found the revolver's holster, plus thirty-five dollars in silver, wrapped in paper from Chestnut's Saloon. A passing soldier pointed out where he had seen a man traveling, probably toward the railroad tracks to the north. Soon, several posses arrived, spreading over a large search area. Meanwhile a telegraph alarm went out from the Havre train station to all terminals and railroad towns across several northern states, and it offered a two-hundred-dollar reward. Soldiers of Fort Assinniboine on nearby field maneuvers searched a several-mile area in all directions. Nothing.

A posse from Fort Benton, led by Sheriff John Buckley, had no better luck. Either the suspect had hitched a wagon ride or he had finally boarded a freight train.

Stevens didn't suffer long from his mortal wounds, and his father came from Stockton, Illinois, for the body. A memorial service for Stevens was held at the First Presbyterian Church. Joined by members of the Fort Assinniboine regimental band, the Havre City Band played. The entire Odd Fellows Lodge put in its appearance, along with members of the American Federation of Labor.

Regionally, authorities captured three "Smiths" in the same week in three different places. Locally, several men were taken into custody, but railroader and handcar operator Ripley couldn't identify any of them. The closest possible clue occurred the following week, when someone fired a shot at a R. Hagen near the infamous Halfway Lake roadhouse. Hagen called the authorities, who conducted a fruitless all-day search.

The Kalispell police alert had described John Smith as being about twenty-four years of age, 5'10", 150 pounds, with light brown hair, a fair complexion, and a smooth-shaven face at the time of his escape. Further, he had small hands, and was well-dressed in new clothes (probably stolen).

Of the reported sightings, the most promising came from St. Croix County, Wisconsin. There, Sheriff Harris had been shot and killed by a man resembling Smith. The sheriff had tried to arrest the man on a train, for robbing a hotel at nearby Roberts. Smith jumped off the train when it slowed to approach the community of Fall Creek. The suspect had ridden the train from St. Paul, and stopped in Roberts across the Mississippi River. He wasn't found. Next came a report from the sheriff of Edwards County, Illinois. It stated that a man in Albion matched Smith's description. The sheriff had dispatched a guard to watch the suspect's mother's home, but he left undiscovered on his bicycle. At Albion he rented a buggy rig, which was later returned by another party. The sheriff thought the man might have been visiting his father. Upon the suspect's return, deputies continued surveillance, but apparently there was no evidence against him other than that he resembled Smith. The last report, soon after Stevens' death, came from Minneapolis, where they had a suspect who called himself Alonga Smith, but he had blond hair. After that, the reports faded.

Meanwhile, the vice campaigns in Havre produced results, closing the ten worst of the two dozen saloons, along with sending the worst of the toughs on their way. James J. Hill was delighted. He awarded Mayor Newman eight hundred miles worth of terminal concessions on the GNR line. Newman operated the one in Havre. Newman later moved his center of business to Great Falls, became mayor and went on to serve in the state legislature. He retired to California a wealthy man.

What happened in the red light district and the roadhouse obviously didn't represent Havre as a whole, although it had a negative effort on the GNR's effort to bring stable, married men to town.

After 1902, the town saw many improvements, including the openings of an opera house and an athletic club, and the expansion of the GNR machine shops to employ 200 men. Even "Shorty" Young got into the act, planting trees around his concert hall along with sweet-peas, hops and cucumber vines (remnants are said to survive at present, along a fence-line). The private park even had a 300-by-800–foot artificial lake that extended north to a levee by the railroad tracks.

The biggest event was the opening of The Fair department store. Not only were the residents happy to see many goods all the way from New York City, but "Shorty's" prostitutes found a good place to shop.

The city's physical plant also made progress with an electric light/steam plant and telephone company. The steam was sent by tunnel all over the downtown. Also, the First Presbyterian Church opened its doors.

Progress was definitely on the march in Havre, thanks to men like Louis Newman and Fred Stevens.

Chinook and Glasgow, 1926

ARMED CONFLICT on town streets didn't always result in deaths. Take the argument of a Patsy Rowle and L. Lopez on the main street of early-day Chinook. Rowle claimed that Lopez owed him $178.00 for shearing sheep. The conversation escalated one day, resulting in Lopez slapping Rowle in the face, and Rowle drew a knife. Lopez grabbed a large rock and club from the street debris, but decided he needed to be armed better, so he went to the hardware store and purchased a revolver.

He returned to the street in order to kill Rowle, but his first two shots went wild, hitting the Montana Hotel window. Finally the third round hit Rowle, and he collapsed in front of the saloon. Lopez was going to finish the job, but bystanders slapped his gun away, with the bullet striking the ground. Lopez went to jail; Rowle spent a few days in the hotel until he recovered. Lopez received a break on the bill since Lopez went to prison.

THEN THERE WAS the Chinook saga of Dan Savage, "aged pioneer" and all-around bad guy, and Charles Smith, town merchant and Blaine County Commissioner. Savage had quarreled with Smith over a business matter for fifteen years. They had previously been involved in what the Chinook newspaper called "pitched battles."

The feud had begun when Savage had refused to pay a bill at Smith's Mercantile, and Smith obtained a court order attaching a bunch of Savage's cattle. Savage had refused to pay the bill because Smith hadn't appointed him town marshal when he was elected mayor. Finally Savage went to prison for trying to kill both Smith and town marshal Granger. Savage received an early parole, and came right back to Harlem to get Smith. Sheriff G.W. Fleming captured Savage after a chase from his house to a ranch on the Missouri River. Upon leaving prison for the second time, Savage bought a gun in Butte before another return to Harlem.

On the Monday morning of September 13, 1926, the two exchanged gunfire just north of the main street and train tracks, near the pool hall, icehouse and Smith's building. Only this morning was different, because Sheriff Fleming had just returned from Glasgow, and he was in Chinook attending a coroner's inquest.

Which was interrupted by several gunshots, and Fleming's quick departure from the courtroom.

This time, Savage carried not only his usual Colt revolver, but also a semi-automatic pistol and several hundred rounds of ammunition. Savage first emptied his revolver at Smith from ambush near the pool hall, and Smith returned the fire. Savage followed up with about eight more rounds from his pistol.

By then the sheriff and a crowd had reached the area—in time to see Savage fleeing west on foot, toward the highway. Smith was unharmed and safe in his house. Fleming procured his car and caught up with Savage in a nearby field just off the highway. The sheriff demanded that Savage stop, but he kept on running, even after the sheriff fired a warning shot in front of him. Fleming's next rifle shot killed Savage. Now another coroner's jury inquest had to be assembled.

But, back to the original coroner's inquest that had summoned Fleming to Chinook.

In Glasgow the sheriff witnessed the arrest of two men for killing another, Eton Shannon, in a Great Northern Railway boxcar at the Paisley Siding, just west of Glasgow. When Sheriff Fleming saw the killer, who was calling himself "Bess," he recognized him as a man named Blackie, whom he had sent to prison for robbing a Chinook store. The man tried to keep out of Fleming's sight, but failed, finally shaking hands with Fleming. The sheriff didn't recognize Bess's companion, A.J. Hill.

The unfolding facts as Fleming heard them began when the I.W.W., Industrial Workers of the World, or Wobblies, sent Shannon out from their Chicago headquarters with a companion named Flood, to find the man or men who were robbing IWW union organizers along the rail line. The IWW, a socialist organization, had its heyday in the earlier mining and timber industries after its 1905 founding, and continues to exist today. Its goal is ending both capitalism and trade unions, with all workers owning all industries, thus employing themselves. In the 1920s, the IWW philosophy fit well into the leftist/socialist mood of far northeastern Montana.

IWW organizers Shannon and Hill had the robbers walk right into their arms at the Paisley Siding, when the two men boarded their boxcar. Shannon demanded to see their IWW cards, saying that otherwise they would not be permitted to board. Both strangers protested, with the shorter one, Bess, drawing his .44 caliber revolver and shooting Shannon. Shannon died shortly after, in the Glasgow hospital. Bess claimed self-defense, but no other gun was found.

A number of IWW members gathered in Glasgow with the avowed intention of hanging Bess/Blackie if he was found innocent. This convinced the suspect that it was safer to plead guilty and go to prison.

Sheriff Fleming, after witnessing that drama, returned to Chinook, and found he might have his own homicide to investigate. A GNR train crew had found a man named Louis Calahan, twenty-two years old, about 300 yards west of the Harlem railroad depot, about midnight on September 12. The body was stretched out along the rail tie ends, one arm against the rail. Calahan's wounds were all in the head. Closer examination showed three distinct gunshot wounds—at the skull base, lower jaw and forehead. The murder angle was dropped when no corroborating evidence could be found. Calahan had been seen drinking earlier on the depot grounds, but his companions had left for a dance at Zurich, about twelve miles to the west. Calahan, authorities learned, disappeared after a single locomotive and passenger car, the "Skidoo," passed through about 10:00 P.M. The coroner's jury eventually decided that Calahan had been hit by that train.

The determination came after an interruption in the hearing, when several gunshots rang out, and Sheriff Fleming had to run to investigate Dan Savage's attack on Charles Smith.

September 1926 supplied a lengthy entry into the crime annals of Milk River Country.

World's Youngest Trick Rider
Miss Doris Ranger, 1914-1984

DORIS RANGER WAS a petite, pretty girl of ninety-five pounds soaking wet, with bobbed blond hair and hazel eyes; she was a veteran trick rider at the age of eight. Her father, "Mose" for Morris, a recognized rodeo performer and horse raiser/trainer, had to shorten the stirrups to accommodate her 5'2" frame. Doris, it is believed, dressed simply for rodeos, usually wearing a man's or western shirt with jodhpur riding pants—loose and full above the knees then close fitting to where they joined the boots. Perhaps her clothing got more elaborate in later years to match that of other women stars, but at first her outfits seemed to copy those of rodeo star Eloise Fox Hastings.

Little Miss Ranger at work. DEBBIE VANDEBERG, HAVRE

Ranger's rodeo performances began with trick riding from the saddle, and later she added roping. She also entered conventional "flat" and relay races, plus at times the roman-riding (standing on a pair of horses) competition. It isn't clear if she ever performed the complete version of the dangerous Russian suicide drag that used no hand-holds, with only one leg over the saddle and hands toward the ground, even though she performed a modified version, holding on with one hand. Perhaps she also performed vault-jumping, over an obstacle while on horseback. About two years into her career, she added jumping over an open Whippet roadster automobile. An unintended version of the trick made quite a stir at Big Horn, Wyoming.

At that rodeo, once she had completed her tricks from the saddle, she started around the track as her father and a helper wheeled the automobile from the infield, placing it perpendicular to the track in front of the grandstand. At her father's signal that the car was properly positioned, she and horse Chubby cut across the infield and started down the track. At the twenty-foot mark, Chubby went into a full gallop, and they leaped into the air as one. That day, the stunt they had done successfully so many times went wrong, ending in what the Sheridan newspaper called, "… an ugly pileup in front of the grandstand." Apparently a rear leg of Chubby's didn't quite clear the automobile. When Doris regained consciousness, the tough child performer stood up and received a standing ovation, before she passed out again.

As the great trick rider Florence Randolph once remarked about accidents, "It's all in the game."

The rodeo where Doris took her spill was a prestigious one: the August 1926 Galatin family Big Horn Riding Association horse festival/dude ranch rodeo that northern Wyoming historian Sam Marton called "the greatest horse festival ever thrown in the history of horse shows." The ranch was located near the community of Big Horn in a created Old West atmosphere in Goose Creek Valley, all situated south of Sheridan in the shadows of the Big Horn Mountains. The event featured the finest in horse flesh, competing in jump and flat races, polo matches, steeple chases, riding show competitions, and many more events. This private rodeo awarded generous cash and merchandise prizes.

The wealthy and prestigious guest ranchers entertained the upper classes of eastern society who spent their summers playing cowboy, since Europe had become "too unsettled" since World War I.

The crowd from twenty-eight different states got to see other exciting mishaps besides Doris's. Ten-year-old Bob Tate—son of R.T. "Red" Tate, a local rodeo talent—leaped off his pony after roping a calf, only to have the animal slip away, with Tate chasing it all over the arena. Instead of Tate's receiving praise, the crowd howled in laughter.

In the relay race, the leader, Emmet Marsh, collided with another rider, causing his saddle cinch to loosen. A third rider seized the moment and pushed Marsh off his horse, resulting in Marsh on the ground, still on his saddle—and only a foot from the finish line! This produced an eight-man fistfight in front of the grandstand. Also, champion Montana rider Paddy Ryan temporarily lost his dignity when a horse bucked him off and he went over the arena fence into a hayfield.

Doris's father joined in the extracurricular activities. The last event of the second day was the quarter-mile race for horses previously ridden in the calf-roping contest. It wasn't one of the larger purse races, but Ranger and a man named Harper got into a dispute anyway. It had to do with the eligibility of their respective horses. The argument ended in Harper "letting his whip fly" at Ranger. The short but wiry Ranger dismounted to face Harper in an unscheduled whipping contest. It ended with Ranger giving his opponent a blow to the face with the butt of his whip, before they were separated.

One hopes the prize money paid for their medical bills.

Father and daughter were back at Big Horn the following year. Unfortunately, as in some rodeos, there was a competitor's weight minimum of 120 pounds that Doris couldn't meet, thus limited her to a fee for trick riding. (Other rodeos had weight minimums as high as 140 pounds.)

Doris Ranger had begun her trick riding career and horse racing career at the ripe old age of eight, starting at her hometown rodeo in Roundup. Her competition career began at age six, when she won the slow-pony race at Roundup. Probably her father's good reputation as a rodeo performer and horse breeder helped Doris break down barriers that might have stopped other talented youngsters. The duo was soon seen on the summer circuit at ranch, town, county, and state fair rodeos.

Trick riding was a daredevil sport that required sheer nerve, combined with the maximum in coordination, timing and stamina—and of course, a great and steady horse. Three women died in this sport before it was changed in 1929 from competition to exhibition-only. How much more ability must a child have needed in this adult sport with their minds and bodies not at full maturity! Obviously it took a great trust in her father's ability to train her. Reportedly, the two had a solid bond that the mother never breached, as Mom had not grown up with horses or ranching.

Doris's rodeo partnership with her father ended in 1931, when she married a Havre cowboy she had met the year before. She and Lee Grant participated in eastern Montana rodeos, touring from Havre, until their oldest child was of school age. Doris also stayed close to her grandfather and father, visiting them frequently in Buffalo, Wyoming.

As to her talent, she apparently never rose above the small and medium rodeos, although she did compete well with champion rodeo stars who frequently played those rodeos between larger ones such as at Cheyenne; Pendleton, Oregon; Calgary, Alberta; Fort Worth; even New York City. It is possible she rode at a young age in the New York City rodeo under the tutelage of top rodeo star Elaine Fox Hastings, and/or briefly toured with a small wild west show, such as Ponca Bill's.

In Havre, Doris was in the shadow of Marie "Ma" Gibson, who established herself a champion bronc and trick rider at major U.S. and Canadian rodeos.

But what sets Doris Ranger apart from the crowd was her performing adult-level trick riding stunts, beginning in the third grade. Thus she was billed as the "World's Youngest Trick Rider."

Life had begun for Doris and twin brother Morris S. on March

14, 1914, when they were born to Morris L. "Mose" Ranger and Dorothy "Dod" Notely-Ranger at Roundup. The seat of Musselshell County, Roundup is forty-six miles north of Billings. It was a typical latter-day western town that grew in a ranching area that evolved into a farming region where some sheep and cattle were raised. An added economic bonus came in the form of the Chicago, Milwaukee, St. Paul and Pacific Railroad. Later development into a major coal-mining region came with the advent of this railroad, known as the "Milwaukee Road."

The Rangers rarely saw Roundup, however, as they lived out on Chimney Butte Ranch, located on Fattig Creek Road in view of the Bull Mountains. Home was a sod cabin with a stone foundation. Fattig Creek flowed north into the Musselshell, which in turn flowed north to the Missouri River. The Ranger family's trading center appeared to be the community of Musselshell on Montana Highway 6 and also on the railroad, east of Roundup. Here were a general store, post office and probably a saloon. The large cattle herds from the southwest United States once crossed the river at this spot. The Musselshell schoolhouse would have been Doris's first contact with larger civilization. It wasn't until the upper school grades that she experienced the bigger town of Roundup, which had about 2,600 people.

Although the area was dotted with sheep and cattle, as well as coal mines, Mose specialized in raising horses, especially racing and polo ponies. Consequently Doris and her brother Morris learned of horses from an early age, helping dad with his business, even delivering horses. While her brother did ranch duties, he apparently didn't have his sister's strong urge to be a rodeo performer. It is unknown whether their mother relished horse-raising, since she came from a working class family in an industrialized section of London, England.

Doris's parents had met when Mose went to England with a wild west show. Mose saw Dod along the parade route, and he stopped to talk to the attractive sixteen-year-old in a pretty white dress. They met again—probably by arrangement—when he returned with a contracted load of polo ponies. They married in England. Dod surely suffered from culture shock upon first viewing her new home in the wide-open, rugged country. (Her sister Beatrice likewise married a cowboy, and moved to northern Wyoming. Perhaps less was more to both.)

The man Dod married was born either at Craig or Choteau, on April 14, 1896. There seems to be confusion as to which of two brothers, Morris and Edwin J., was born where. Mose's parents were Edwin "Ishi" Ranger and Susan Tubbs Ranger. The settlement of Craig, located on the Missouri River between Great Falls and Helena, was a small train stop on the Great Northern Railway.

Edwin Ranger, Doris's grandfather, had come from a family on Long Island, New York, and had been educated partially in Europe. He ventured to Montana in 1886, engaging in the stock raising business near Choteau and possibly Billings. His obituary stated he had worked for the Canadian Pacific Railroad near Calgary, Alberta, and joined the gold rush to the Klondike (circa 1898) in the Yukon Territory.

The 1900 U.S. Census also showed Edwin living on the Crow Indian Reservation in southeastern Montana, perhaps running a store. By 1920, he had a general store at Roundup. After Edwin and Susan divorced, she moved to California and he settled in Buffalo, Wyoming. Edwin may have been attracted by the strong Spanish-American War veterans' organization there and/or the local Masonic order. The Buffalo area also had a veterans' home at old Fort McKinney, and a veterans' hospital at Sheridan.

Edwin served in the Spanish American War with one of the three volunteer regiments of future President Theodore "Teddy" Roosevelt's Rough Riders—possibly Wyoming's 2nd US Volunteer Cavalry. Edwin flourished in Buffalo, acquiring a substantial home and other properties, and serving as justice of the peace.

Apparently the elder Ranger's livestock business created a cowboy, horseman, and rodeo performer in son Mose. His grandson Jeff Ranger remembered seeing a picture of Mose in an old horseman's magazine, celebrating his talents. Unfortunately, Mose's marriage was doomed with his many travels of delivering horses, training Hollywood actors and horses, or following the rodeo circuit as a rider, coach, and gambler.

After divorcing him, Dod moved to the Arvada, Wyoming, area, where her brother-in-law, Stanley Collins, lived. (Dod's sister Beatrice had died, leaving Stanley a family to raise.) Youngest daughter (by two years) Grace moved to California to live with her grandmother Susan.

Mose and daughter Doris moved to Buffalo with her Grandfather Edwin.

The Ranger family moved in with Edwin at his Buffalo home. It was located on the far north end of town, apparently close to the main cattle trail. Young Morris and Doris began high school, with Doris and father Mose following the rodeo circuit in the summer. Mose spent the rest of the year raising horses somewhere in the area, perhaps on one of Edwin's other properties. He also operated a gambling den in the back of a local saloon.

Young Morris, influenced by Edwin, would finish high school and go to college at the University of Wyoming. His career of both white- and blue-collar jobs spanned the West, including Alaska. He eventually settled in Helena, working for Mountain Bell Telephone Company. Grace moved from California to Las Vegas, where she was in the entertainment industry.

DORIS'S NEW HOME of Buffalo was on the east side of the Big Horn Mountains on rolling plains and hills; the town approximated the size of Roundup. A waterway through town, Clear Creek, flows into the Powder River near the Montana state line. The town's main street supposedly followed an old buffalo trail, with its local destination being the famous Occidental Hotel and Saloon.

Buffalo had been at the heart of the 1885 Johnson County War, when large-scale cattle ranchers tried to run out farmers and small-scale ranchers. A side effect for Buffalo was that the powerful Wyoming Stock Growers Association labeled the town the "rustlers' capital" of Wyoming. WSGA's great influence on state government helped it to prevent the railroad from building a depot and cattle-loading stop at Buffalo, crippling the town's development.

A few years before he and his daughter moved to Buffalo, Mose had launched Doris's rodeo career beyond Roundup, at Billings' Midland Empire Fair and Rodeo in September of 1923. He didn't initially bill her as the world's youngest trick rider, but simply as Doris Ranger, eight-year-old trick rider. The Billings fair-rodeo may have been the largest at the time in Montana.

Located on the Yellowstone River, the city was a major trading/distribution/shipping center for a large portion of eastern Montana and northeastern Wyoming, thanks in part to its large Northern Pacific Railroad presence. It could even boast of two colleges. The local chamber of commerce proclaimed that "a tiny frontier trading post and cowtown became a metro-political area overnight with an area as large as New York City."

The September 9, 1923, *Billings Gazette* gave Doris the better part of a page to introduce her to their rodeo enthusiasts. It featured two pictures, one a portrait, the other of her performing on her horse. The caption stated that she would be performing "many fancy and difficult riding stunts daily before the grandstand." It went on to explain that she was the daughter of Mose Ranger, "well known Montana rider." Lastly it printed a letter to a Mr. Shoemaker, presumably a fair official. It read:

Roundup, Montana
August 26, 1923

Dear Mr. Shoemaker:

I am Doris Ranger, my twin brother Morris and I were born in Roundup 8 years ago. We went to the ranch on Fattig Creek when we were babies and we've always lived there until last fall when we came to town to go to school. We went to a country school one year. I liked that best because we rode our ponys two miles and we ran races every day. We are in the third grade now. I don't like school very much except writing. I love to write. I've had Cutie, my pony, four years. Daddy brought him home in the wagon one night, he was lying down with his feet tied up and I thought he was a big puppy. When I first started to ride him he bucked me off every morning but he's a good boy now. He can do lots of tricks. Cutie and I are going to ride at your fair this year and we are tickled to death. Cuties is going to wear a red ribbon. I rode in the slow pony race in Roundup when I was six, I beat. If I didn't have to wash dishes and dust and study my lessons I would ride eavry minit. Mama said I could write anything I wanted to but only one page. I hope you like my picture. My to front teeth were out all winter. I am awful glad they grew in before the picture was tooken.

Yours Truly,
Doris Ranger

It wouldn't be much of a stretch to surmise that her letter and pictures would win over the hearts and minds of her soon-to-be audience. Besides trick riding, Doris would participate in the women's relay and other races. As usually was the case, she entered the relay race against stiff competition from such seasoned adults as Mrs. Floyd Kronkright and Dannetta Gilbert. The relay race required three changes of horses with the same saddle. Each contestant was allowed one helper/horse-holder, who in her case, would have been her father. Doris was disqualified at another rodeo when a second helper jumped in.

Doris came in third every time, yet only a few seconds behind; however, the newspaper reported that "she was soundly applauded for her pluck."

Her father tried steer wrestling and roping, but came up short. This apparently finished his career in steer wrestling, but at age twenty-seven he was still good at calf roping, flat racing, and the roman race. In spite of some failures, it had been a good day for them, with no accidents marring their performances.

Doris returned the following year to Billings, performing her trick riding and competing in races. She again found Dannetta Gilbert to be in the relay race. Gilbert and her husband rarely met defeat in regional rodeos. Little Doris Ranger again came in third, but again received the most applause. A bonus came when she was filmed for a travelogue publicizing the fair/rodeo.

Now billed as the youngest trick rider in the world, she continued to perform in the Midland Empire rodeo through at least 1926, before she and he father moving to Buffalo. Doris also introduced a trick: jumping his horse over an Overland Whippet Roadster with its top down. At times she gave an exhibition or raced in the roman race, astride two horses.

She had introduced the new car stunt at her hometown of Roundup. Unfortunately the smaller towns couldn't always afford a yearly rodeo because of the tough economic times. Roundup's bank closed, the town couldn't afford to keep the library open, and the flour mill burned down. In 1926, though, Roundup and its American Legion post put on an exceptional rodeo. Doris introduced the car jump and gave an exhibition of her roman-riding, but allowed another rider, Marvin Guptil, to ride her horses, Cutie and Smartie, to victory in the actual race. Doris did enter the Half Mile special running race on Lucky Star, and beat out her male competition. However, she didn't test Mrs. Gilbert in the other races. Mose rode Lucky Star in the three-eights open race, but finished in third place. As part of the grandstand entertainment, a local acrobatic team performed, one of its members being the elder Ranger daughter, Grace. Grace wasn't into ranching or rodeos.

Doris would join her father on the rodeo circuit from late spring into October, or as the school schedule allowed. The father-daughter duo followed a regional circuit of state fairs, county fairs, and town and ranch rodeos. They reportedly traveled in a rented railroad boxcar with their horses. Doris later commented to nephew Jeff Ranger she enjoyed looking out the car's door at sunrise. Because of the tough economic times and harsh weather conditions affecting farms, ranches and towns, the rodeo life of the 1920s and '30s was not easy.

Nevertheless, northern Wyoming provided a good opportunity with three consecutive rodeos at Big Horn, Buffalo, and Sheridan. Sheridan and Sheridan County put on the biggest rodeo in northern Wyoming, and claimed to be the second-best in the state, surpassed by only Cheyenne Frontier Days. Big Horn and Buffalo offered competitive cash and merchandise prizes.

The Chicago, Burlington and Quincy Railroad—"The Burlington Route"—had come to Sheridan in 1892, having passed by Buffalo because of its false outlaw reputation, and its would continually increase its Sheridan presence. The town of 8,500 had all the amenities to be a first class city: a hospital, radio station, two movie theaters, a swimming pool, parks, golf course, tennis courts, etc. Industries included a sugar beet factory, flour mill, cereal mill, livestock feedlots, brewery, ice plant, iron foundry, brick-and-tile plant, creameries, newspapers—and a regional coal mining industry. The bus line connected with Billings to the north and Casper to the south. The airport offered national connections, and a taxi to and from the town. In addition, there was the summer influx of wealthy easterners who came to play cowboy at the many dude ranches.

Doris participated in Sheridan/Sheridan County rodeos from 1924 to at least 1928. She continued being billed as "the youngest trick rider in the world." She followed the pattern of running in the women's relay race, and the men's if there was no weight requirement, as well as doing her trick riding. She continued to lose races against Dannetta Gilbert and other veterans until 1927, when she began riding a horse called "Chubby." With this horse she finished second in the relay and first in the quarter-mile race.

The 1927 rodeo in her new home of Buffalo was a good one for Doris. The *Buffalo Bulletin* included her picture, advertising her stunt riding as part of its general coverage. Doris rode in the half-mile free-for-all race, taking first place against male competition. She finished in second place in the half-mile race against reigning local champion Ray Barkey, although she had bested Barkey in her first race. Mose came in second against Barkey in the roman standing race. That day, Doris rode a horse called Popeye.

The 1928 Johnson County Rodeo had great weather, many contestants, and record attendance—6,000 people, which filled all the seats. Doris did trick riding and now roping.

On the first day of the fair, Doris won the half-mile race for saddle horses—against male competitors. The next day, the crowd saw the pair win the three-eights-mile saddle race. The third day, she won the half-mile roman race, against men who included her father. Mose, riding Popeye and Red Cloud for the event, repeated his last year's second-place finish.

Apparently, since Doris's tricks were getting more complicated, she raced on Chubby, and used other Ranger horses for the trick act.

The glory of these wins faded the following month at the Wyoming State Fair, held in Douglas. During the women's relay race, a pile-up occurred when Doris's horse stumbled on the back stretch; next a horse directly behind Chubby stumbled over the fallen animal and threw its rider, a Mrs. Carmin. Carmin suffered a sprained wrist and serious body bruising. A woman named Nancy Hudson joined the pile-up, landing under her horse and dying from a concussion. No information was given on Doris or Chubby's condition.

Previous to the mishap, Doris had placed second in the mile dash, and third in a heat of the women's relay race against Mrs. Carmin and a Mrs. Walker.

The 1929 Buffalo–Johnson County fair-rodeo topped the previous year's attendance, again with support from Sheridan merchants and residents. Mose took to the saddle, and competed against Ray Barkey, who usually won the all-event winner's award. Barkey bested Mose Ranger in the mule novelty race, although

Mose won against him in the reserve race. Mose finished third in the mule running-race, while Doris lost out against Dannetta Gilbert in the half-mile race. Doris came in second against male competition in the quarter-mile running-race heat, but won it on the third day.

Unfortunately there is no known scrapbook or diary to tell us what the Ranger father-and-daughter summer schedule entailed, and research efforts are hindered because not all rodeos published the results, or at least not for the women's races. "A good time was had by all" summarized these rodeos. Doris didn't participate in the Miles City Roundup, although she did ride in other Montana rodeos. There are no newspapers to review for the important Wolf Point Stampede. For sure, she never participated in the top-level Cheyenne Frontier Days, although Mose may have at a younger age.

Apparently life during the school year at Buffalo was good for Doris. She had a close relationship with her brother, father and grandfather. School must have gone well, too, because she was one of two sports cheerleaders at her high school as a sophomore. Nineteen-thirty was the first year the student body chose them. The *Wyomalo* yearbook shows both the cheerleaders' pictures in a 1931 group picture.

The late summer of 1930 found Mose and Doris in north-central Montana's Milk River Country at the Havre and Chinook county fair rodeos. At sixteen, Doris obviously could no longer be billed as Little Miss Ranger or the youngest trick rider in the world now, so she was just plain Doris Ranger, trick roper and trick rider.

Chinook was a typical small ranching/farming town along the Great Northern Railway; at the time the town had a sugar beet factory and the surrounding fields of beets, plus crops of potatoes, alfalfa, oats, wheat, and barley and other grains.

At the town's 1930 rodeo, Mose participated in the roman-riding race, but lost to Edna Bell of Wolf Point, and local favorite, Steven Adams Jr. Doris won the women's relay race, with Edna Bell close behind. The *Chinook Opinion* newspaper called Bell one of the best-known riders and breeders in the state, saying she brought some rather swift steeds. Unfortunately, Bell remains an unsung hero, with no recognition in historical rodeo records.

A young fellow named Lee Grant finished second in the men's relay-race, behind Steve Adams Jr. Of course Doris did her trick riding during the two afternoon shows. Mose did better in Havre without Edna Bell to compete against, winning the roman race, and Doris won the quarter-mile horse race on Chubby, with Bell right behind. Doris and Lee Grant met again, which only enhanced their mutual attraction.

Lee Grant said Mose skipped the Havre event in 1931 to avoid any further romantic developments between his daughter and the young man. Doris had originally been scheduled to perform, advance publicity billing her as "the Wyoming artist who presents her rope twitching and trick riding." It is quite possible that Lee's memory was correct, since no mention is made of her performance at the rodeo's conclusion, only the clown and high wire acts.

However, the two met anyway at the Blaine County–Chinook fair-rodeo in spite of Mose's best effort to thwart Cupid. Doris again performed her trick riding and roping for two afternoons, yet there is no mention of the Rangers or Lee Grant participating in any competitions.

Next the Rangers were scheduled for the Valley County fair-rodeo in Glasgow, as they followed their regional rodeo circuit. At season's end, Lee and Doris married in Havre's Van Orsdel United Methodist Church, on November 13, 1931. Doris gave her age as nineteen instead of the actual seventeen. Granddaughter Debbie Vandeberg explained that Doris's age had been inflated to qualify her for rodeos during the early years, and she left it that way.

Now Lee had a wife to support, hence following the rodeo circuit and living in stables wouldn't do. Certainly Mose was upset about his daughter's future, besides missing an important part of his family.

The young cowboy's family had come west from Illinois to take up a homestead in southern Saskatchewan. They first settled in the Govenlock area, just north of the border from Havre, but moved to the Havre area about 1926, and subsequently operated two ranches, a hotel and a dairy. At the time Lee met Doris there wasn't any employment for him. Times were tough during the "dirty thirties," with dismal farm prices and infestation of crickets and grasshoppers. He found ranching work at the Saskatchewan town of Robsart, a few miles northwest of Govenlock. This may have become a Grant family ranch, also. On the trip there, the couple braved frigid weather and a blizzard. Fortunately, they found a rancher's line shack for shelter on the prairie.

The next day, breakfast consisted of oatmeal with mouse droppings in it. Unfortunately the pack horse had died overnight, adding to their troubles. Behind their former north Havre home are metal sculptures they installed to depict that trip.

The family returned to Havre, where Lee did ranch work and various jobs at Star Billiards and Havre Hotel, until he got a full-time position with the Great Northern Railway in 1935.

Lee produced the area's first night-time rodeo at Gildford, in 1933. Local stars Marie Gibson and Lawrence Green helped make it a success. Unfortunately, the receipts disappeared, and Lee's rodeo friends were robbed at a local hotel.

Doris and Lee also continued on a limited rodeo circuit, even taking along their now two children, Nancy and Gary. Nancy, being the elder, got the task of watching Gary while their parents rode, at least until she was of school age. Nancy still vividly remembers a 1938 High-Line rodeo where Doris's horse bucked when the starting gate opened, and Doris hit her head on the gate's pipe frame. The horse took off, dragging Doris with one foot in the stirrup. Nancy watched in horror as the ambulance pulled up and her mother was placed on a stretcher. She had forgotten Gary, running to her mother's side. Doris's face was a ghostly white, she recalls—along with being spanked for leaving Gary alone in the stands!

The couple's north Havre home started life as a boxcar—a step above a stable—and the rest of the house was built to encompass it. When Gary Grant was married in 1952, his parents bought a home a block away on 6th Street North, a house they had always wanted. Gary and his family moved into the old house.

Lee went to work full-time on the railroad as a brakeman, and Doris found a new hobby, knitting, which she turned into a business. First she used a space in Gary's upholstery shop, next she moved to a cubbyhole in the downtown Super Ice Cream building, and lastly sold from a room of their home. She also worked as a night clerk at the Shanty Motel, which included a restaurant and bar. Granddaughters remember being treated with meals there and swimming in the motel pool. At their home, they had a small stable where they kept two horses. Lee said he would make rodeo stars out of the granddaughters, but they had no interest.

Retired Havre reference librarian Francine Brady often visited Doris with her mother, Pauline Krezelak. Brady remembers Doris as a thin woman with lots of stamina and many friends. Doris told Francine she had injured her stomach in a rodeo accident and could eat only a small portion of food at one time. Cigarettes and coffee were her mainstay. Doris was an excellent cook, and she shared many of her recipes. Pauline used Doris's divinity recipe—and it never failed.

Doris's later life definitely centered on her grandchildren, who lived just down the street and visited regularly. Librarian Francine also remembers Doris caring for granddaughter Debbie when the child was in a body cast, allowing Gary's wife to care for their other children. Doris would be seen carrying Debbie or pushing her in a wheelchair.

Doris did get a treat from heaven, however, when Gary Grant's youngest daughter, Lori, married a rancher's son, David Kanning, from Galata. They now they live down Shepherd Road, east of the old Grant place near the Milk River. Their daughter, Lauren, took to horses (under her father's influence), and became a barrel racer. Lauren went to Montana State University at Bozeman on a rodeo scholarship. She finished college at Tarleton State University at Stephensville, Texas. Today she no longer races, yet continues her close rodeo association by being a marketing representative for Classic Equine ranch and rodeo horse gear.

Mose Ranger continued to live in Buffalo at his father's home. Edwin died in 1943, at the age of seventy-six, at the VA Hospital near Sheridan. Mose apparently converted the house into several small apartments. He continued his carefree style of life with wine, women and song, until he came to live with the Grant family after having developed health problems. He died of a heart attack in 1958, upon returning from the Mayo Clinic in Rochester, Minnesota.

Doris Ranger Grant died in 1984 at the age of sixty-nine, leaving a legacy of crocheters and knitters, including family members, around the greater Havre area. She also left a legacy of love—caring for her family being a priority, probably because of her memories of her parents' split.

Although her obituary mentioned she had been a trick rider on the rodeo circuit, it failed to mention that she once starred as "Little Miss Doris Ranger, the youngest trick rider in the world."

ALTHOUGH NOT AS well known nationally as some, Doris Ranger joined the pantheon of early women rodeo riders who risked life and limb to amaze and delight eager crowds at local, regional and national rodeos. She shared this honor locally with Marie "Ma" Gibson, who was a constant winner at rodeos of all sizes. Statewide, Doris was in the company of Fanny Sperry Steele, Alice and Margie Greenough, the Getts sisters, Christine Synnes, Violet Keagle, Edna Bell, and others.

Today, women are restricted to Professional Rodeo Cowboys Association barrel racing competitions—unless they enter rodeos produced by the Women's Professional Rodeo Association, where prize money is modest. However, this hasn't slowed women down. On March 1, 1992, Charmayne James Rodman, then a nine-time national barrel racing champion, won $18,546 at a Houston rodeo. This set a new world's record for any male or female in any single event.

Candi Zion Solomon continues that tradition of excellence. The Great Falls native has been involved in raising show horses, championship barrel racing, promoting rodeos, training future stars, and now breeds barrel-racing horses.

The women of rodeo probably would not have considered themselves early feminists, just women of independent thoughts, ways and deeds.

According to author Teresa Jordan,

> The West was never an easy place for a woman. Loneliness, isolation and hard work took its toll in neuralgia, insanity and long and lingering illnesses. But many women prospered in the West. Some of these were cowgirls, who found their answers to these problems by working outside. Through a combination of necessity, circumstance and determination, they made a place for themselves in the larger world of horses, cows and men…

Bibliography

Introduction

Hufstetler, Mark. Fort Assinniboine, MT. Historic and Architectural Overview. Havre, 1989-90.

Knight, Oliver. *Life and Manners in the Frontier Army* (Norman: University of Oklahoma Press, 1978).

Roe, Frances M.A. *Army Letters from an Officer's Wife* (New York: Appleton, 1909).

Scott, Kim Allen. *Yellowstone Denied: The Life of Gustavus Cheyney Doane* (Norman: University of Oklahoma Press, 2007).

Army Chaplain's Wife

Dodd, Eliza Shaw. "Diary at Fort Assinniboine 1881-1883."

Fort Assiniboine Preservation Society Archives, Havre, MT.

Hufstetler, Mark. "Fort Assinniboine, MT: Historic and Architectural overview, Havre, 1989-90."

Knight, Oliver. *Life and Manners in the Frontier Army.* Norman: University of Oklahoma Press, 1978.

Roe, Frances M.A. *Army Letters from an Officer's Wife.* New York: Appleton, 1909.

Scott, Kim Allen. *Yellowstone Denied: The Life of Gustavus Cheyney Doane.* Norman: University of Oklahoma Press, 2007.

U.S. Census of 1880.

Wilson, Gary A. Personal research collection.

Métis Prince of the Plains
Dempsey, Hugh A. *Big Bear: The End of Freedom.* Lincoln: University of Nebraska Press, Bison Book, 1986.

Howard, Joseph Kinsey. *Strange Empire: A Narrative of the Northwest.* St. Paul: Minnesota Historical Society, 1994 reprint.

Lalonds, Meika, and Elton La Clare. *Discover Saskatchewan: A Guide to Historic Sites.* Regina, Sask.: Canadian Plains Research Center, University of Regina, 1998.

Mulvaney, Charles Pelham, M.D. *The Métis Rebellion of 1885.* Toronto: Coles Publishing Co., reprint 1971.

Pelletier, Joanne. *Gabriel Dumont.* Regina, Sask.: Gabriel Dumont Institute of Native Studies and Applied Research, Inc., 1985.

Woodcock, George. *Gabriel Dumont: The Métis Chief and His Lost World.* Edmonton, Alta.: Hurtig Publisher, 1976.

Two Legendary Missionaries
Allison, Janet S. *Trial and Triumph: 101 Years in North Central Montana.* Chinook, MT: North Central Montana Cowbelles, 1968.

Beal, Merrill D. *I Will Fight No More Forever: Chief Joseph and the Nez Perce War.* New York: Ballantine Books, 1976.

Burlingame, Merrill G. *The Montana Frontier.* Bozeman: Big Sky Books, 1980.

Byren, Stacey. "Following in Brother Van's Footprints." *Great Falls (MT) Tribune,* June 1, 2008.

Chaney, Roberta Carkeek. *Names on the Face of Montana.* Missoula: Mountain Press Publishing Co., 1983.

Joseph Kinsey Howard, *Montana Margins: A State Anthology* (New Haven: Yale University Press, 1946).

History Committee, Doris J. Franzen, Chairman. *Footprints in the Valley.* 3 vols. Glasgow MT, 1987.

Lavender, David. *Bent's Fort.* Lincoln: University of Nebraska Press, Bison Book, 1972.

Lind, Robert W. *Brother Van: Montana Pioneer Circuit Rider.* Las Vegas, NV: privately published in cooperation with Skyhouse Publishers, Helena, MT, 1972.

McAstocker, David. *My Ain Laddie.* Boston: The Stratford Publishing Co., 1922.

Noyes, Alfred. *In the Land of Chinook: The History of Blaine County.* Helena, MT: State Publishing Company, 1917.

Joel Overholser. *Fort Benton: World's Innermost Port.* Privately published in cooperation with Falcon Press Publishing Co., Inc., Helena, MT, 1987.

Schoenberg, Wilfred P., S.J. *Jesuits in Montana*. Portland, OR: The Oregon-Jesuit, 1960.

Sedacek, Signe N., Chairwoman. *Grit, Guts & Gusto: A History of Hill County*. Havre: The Hill County Bicentennial Commission, 1976.

Ranch Woman Extraordinaire

Abbott, E.C. ("Teddy Blue"), and Helen Huntington Smith. *We Pointed Them North: Recollections of a Cow Puncher*. Norman: University of Oklahoma Press, 1955.

Allison, Janet S. *Trial and Triumph: 100 Years in North Central Montana*. Chinook: North Central Montana Cow Belles, 1968.

Bryan, William L. Jr. *Montana's Indians: Yesterday and Today*. Helena: American World Geographic Publishing, 1996.

Howard, Joseph Kinsey. *Strange Empire: A Narrative of the Northwest*. St. Paul: Minnesota Historical Society, 1994 reprint.

Lucke, Mary Evelyn. *Margaret* [Faber]. Havre, MT: Privately published, 1983.

Lalonds, Meika, and Elton La Clare. *Discover Saskatchewan: A Guide to Historic Sites*. Regina, Sask.: Canadian Plains Research Center, University of Regina, 1998.

Noyes, A.J. *In the Land of Chinook, or, The Story of Blaine County*. Helena: State Publishing Co., 1917.

Shirley, Gayle C. *More Than Petticoats*. Helena, MT: Two Dot Imprint of Globe-Pequot Press, 1995.

Wilson, Gary A. *Long George Francis: Gentleman Outlaw of Montana*. Helena, MT: Two Dot Imprint of Globe-Pequot Press, 2005.

Two Cattle Queens

Allison, Janet S. *Trial and Triumph: 100 Years in North Central Montana*. Chinook, MT: North Central Montana Cowbelles, 1968.

Cheney, Roberta Carkeek. *Names on the Face of Montana*. Rev. ed. Missoula: Mountain Press Publishing Co., 1984.

Jordan, Teresa. *Cowgirls of the American West*. Garden City, NY: Anchor Press, 1982.

Ranstrom, Barbara, and Dan Friede. *Chinook: The First Hundred Years*. Montana: Chinook Centennial 89ers, Inc.

U.S. Census, Population Data 1920 and 1930, Seattle and Renton, WA.

Wallace, Charles. *The Cattle Queen of Montana: A Story of the Personal Experiences of Mrs. Nate Collins*. St. James, MN: Charles, Forte, 1894.

Great Warrior of the Gros Ventres Tribal Wars
Bryan, William L. Jr. *Montana's Indians: Yesterday and Today*. Helena: American World Geographic Publishing, 1996.

Chittenden, Hiram Martin. *The American Fur Trade of the Far West*. New York: The Press of the Pioneers, 1935.

Dixon, Joseph K. *The Vanishing Race: The Last Great Indian Council*. New York: Bonanza Books, 1963 reprint.

Ewers, John C. *The Blackfeet: Raiders on the Northwestern Plains*. Norman: University of Oklahoma Press, 1958.

Ewers, John C. *Ethnological Report on The Blackfeet and Gros Ventre Tribes of Indian Lands in Northern Montana*. Smithsonian Institution, circa 1953.

Flannery, Regina. *The Gros Ventres of Montana*. Part I. Washington, D.C.: The Catholic University of American Press, 1975 reprint.

Gone, Fred P., ed. by George Horse Capture. *The Seven Visions of Bull Lodge, as Told by his Daughter, Garter Snake*. Lincoln: University of Nebraska Press, 1992 reprint.

Miller, Don, and Stan Cohen. *Military and Trading Posts of Montana*. Missoula, MT: Pictorial Histories Publishing Co., 1978.

Smah, Dennis J., et al. *The History of the Fort Peck Assiniboine and Sioux Tribes, 1800-2000*. Fort Peck, MT, 2008.

Utley, Robert M. *Frontier Regulars: The United States Army and the Indians, 1866-1890*. New York: MacMillan Publishing Co., 1973.

Wellington, J. W. "Duke," "The Legendary Medicine Bundle of Red Whip, Gros Ventre Warrior," *Montana Magazine*, July-August 1982.

The Travels of an Outlaw's Widow
Buckley, Phil, Harlem, MT. Letter to Stacey W. Osgood, Chicago, September 11, 1960.

Horan, James D. *Desperate Men: Revelations from the Sealed Pinkerton Files*. New York: Doubleday & Company, 1949.

Landusky, Julia. "The Days of Old, The Days of Gold." From an article in *Paradise (CA) News*.

Logan, Cinderilla Athanissa "Elfie" Dessery. Biographical notes transcribed from shorthand notes taken by daughter-in-law Edith Moran in Le Canada, CA, circa 1958.

Powell, C.W., Whitefish, MT, letter to J.J. Brannan, Ocean Beach, CA. March 24, 1938.

Waller, Brown. *Last of the Great Western Train Robbers.* New York: A/S Barnes and Co., 1968.

Wilson, Gary A. *Tiger of the Wild Bunch: The Life and Death of Harvey "Kid Curry" Logan.* Guilford, CT: Globe Pequot Press, Two Dot imprint, 2000.

Milk River Angel of Mercy

Allison, Janet S. *Trial and Triumph: 100 Years in North Central Montana.* Chinook: North Central Montana Cow Belles, 1968.

Bronson, Earl J. "Early Day Montana Nurse Thora Phalen, Tended Sick in Cuba, Minnesota and Washington," *Havre (MT) Daily News,* February 4, 1966.

Cheney, Roberta Carkeek. *Names on the Face of Montana.* Rev. ed. Missoula: Mountain Press Publishing Co., 1984.

Hagener, Louis W. & Antoinette R. Hagener. *A Northern Reflection.* Rev. ed. Havre, MT: Northern Alumni Association, 2001.

Phalen, Thora. "Havre at the Beginning of the Century," in Havre Chamber of Commerce, *Semi-Annual Report of Havre Chamber of Commerce,* 1950.

Sedacek, Signe N., Chairwoman. *Grit, Guts & Gusto: A History of Hill County.* Havre: The Hill County Bicentennial Commission, 1976.

Steele, Volney, M.D. *Bleed, Blister and Purge: A History of Medicine on the American Frontier.* Missoula: Montana Press Publishing Company, 2005.

Undated clipping, article on Thora Phalen, found among personal items of her granddaughter Jane Trotchie, Havre, MT.

Journeying to & Living at the Fort in the 1880s

Broadwater, Kathlyn. "Early Days of Fort Assinniboine." Parts I-III. *Havre Daily News,* January, 1933.

Broadwater-Blanchard-McCulloh family history. Author's collection.

Bryan, William L. Jr. *Montana's Indians: Yesterday and Today.* Helena: American World Geographic Publishing, 1996.

"Memoirs of Mary Wickham Kellogg." Elinor Clack, former curator of the Clack Museum, Havre, MT, found the manuscript in the possession of grandson Joe Urschal of Saratoga, FL. Also in Clack's research materials are various versions of manuscripts typed by Clack, and research notes on Fort Assinniboine history materials. Author's collection.

Frazer, Robert W. *Forts of the West.* Norman: University of Oklahoma Press, 1972.

"Hardships of a Frontier Post: Mrs. Robert L. McCulloh of Lee's Summit Was the Wife of a Freighter at Fort Assinniboine, Mont.," *Kansas City (MO) Star*, April 12, 1931.

Lawrence, Mary Leafe; ed. by Thomas T. Smith. *Daughter of the Regiment.* Lincoln: University of Nebraska Press, 1972.

Madsen, Betty, and Brigham D. *North to Montana! Jehus, Bullwhackers and Mule Skinners on the Montana Trail.* Logan: Utah State University Press, 1998.

The "Lost" Marias Pass

Albro, Martin. *James J. Hill and The Opening of the Northwest.* New York: Oxford University Press, 1976.

Federal Writers' Project. *Montana: A State Guide Book.* New York: Hastings House, 1939, reprint 1946.

Sedacek, Signe N., Chairwoman. *Grit, Guts & Gusto: A History of Hill County.* Havre: The Hill County Bicentennial Commission, 1976.

Wilson, Gary A. "The Search for the Legendary "Lost" Marias Pass. *Havre (MT) Daily News*, August 7, 1983.

Lambert & Its Lady Rodeo Performer

Cheney, Roberta Carkeek. *Names on the Face of Montana.* Rev. ed. Missoula: Mountain Press Publishing Co., 1984.

Federal Writers' Project. *Montana. A State Guide Book.* New York: Hastings House, 1939, reprint 1946.

Presser, Marvin. *Wolf Point: City of Destiny.* Billings, MT: MSU Press, 1997.

Stiffler, Liz & Toni Blake. "Fannie Sperry-Steele: Montana's Champion Bronc Rider." *Montana: The Magazine of Western History*, Spring, 1982.

Stout, Tom, ed. "O.H. Cronkright" in *Montana: Its Story and Biography.* Chicago: The American Historical Society, 1921.

Blood on the Trail

William L. Bryan Jr., *Montana's Indians: Yesterday and Today* (Helena: American & World Geographic, 1996).

Dodd, Eliza Shaw. Diary at Fort Assinniboine 1881-1883. Archives, Fort Assiniboine Preservation Association, Havre, MT.

Federal Writers' Project. *Montana: A State Guide Book.* New York: Hastings House, 1939; reprint 194.

Fort Belknap log of Major William H. Fenton, trader. 1873-1875. Author's collection.

Glasgow Jubilee Committee. Ed. by Vivian A. Paladin. *From Buffalo Bones to Sonic Boom.* Glasgow Jubilee Committee, 1962.

The History Committee. Ed. by Frazen, Doris. *Footprints in Valley County.* Volumes 1-3. Glasgow, 1990.

Hufstetler, Mark. *Fort Assinniboine, MT: Historic and Architectural Overview.* Havre, 1989-90.

Parks Canada. *Batoche: National Historic Site of Canada.* 2005.

Allen Scott, Kim Allen. *Yellowstone Denied: The Life of Gustavus Cheyney Doane* (Norman: University of Oklahoma Press, 2007).

Sedacek, Signe N., Chairwoman. *Grit, Guts & Gusto: A History of Hill County.* Havre: The Hill County Bicentennial Commission, 1976.

Smith, Helena Huntington. *The War on Powder River: The History of an Insurrection.* Lincoln: University of Oklahoma Press, Bison Book, 1966.

Toole, K Ross. *Montana: An Uncommon Land.* Norman: University of Oklahoma Press, 1955.

Wilson, Gary A. *Tiger of the Wild Bunch: The Life and Death of Harvey "Kid Curry" Logan.* Guilford, CT: Globe Pequot Press, Two Dot imprint, 2000.

World's Youngest Trick Rider

Allison, Janet S. *Trial and Triumph: 100 Years in North Central Montana.* Chinook: North Central Montana Cow Belles, 1968.

Bryan, William L. Jr. *Montana's Indians: Yesterday and Today.* Helena: American World Geographic Publishing, 1996.

Cheney, Roberta Carkeek. *Names on the Face of Montana.* Rev. ed. Missoula: Mountain Press Publishing Co., 1984.

Dawson, Patrick. *Mr. Rodeo: The Big Bronc Years of Leo Cramer.* Livingston, MT: Cayuse Press, 1986.

Federal Writers' Project. *Montana. A State Guide Book.* New York: Hastings House, 1939, reprint 1946.

Federal Writers' Project. *Wyoming: A Guide to Its History, Highways and People.* Lincoln: University of Nebraska Press, Bison Edition, 1981.

Frazer, Robert W. *Forts of the West.* Norman: University of Oklahoma Press, 1965.

Giebel, Doug. *In Print: Havre, MT, Volume One, 1807-1904.* Havre: Doug Giebel and the Performing Art Group, 1987.

Holland, William C., Chairman. *Buffalo's First Century.* Buffalo's Centennial Book Committee, 1984.

Jordan, Teresa. *Cowgirls: Women of the American West, An Oral History.* Garden City, NY: Anchor Press, 1982.

Le Compte, Mary Lou. *Cowgirls of the Rodeo*. Urbana: University of Illinois Press, 1993.

McGinnis, Vern. *Rodeo Road: My Life as a Pioneer Cowgirl*. New York: Hastings House, 1974.

Miller, Don, and Stan Cohen. *Military and Trading Posts of Montana*. Missoula, MT: Pictorial Histories Publishing Co., 1978.

Morten, Sam. *Where the Rivers Run North*. Sheridan, WY: Sheridan County Historical Society Press, 2007.

Raymer, Robert George. *Montana: Its Story and Biography*. Volume I. Chicago: The American Historical Society, 1921.

Roach, Joyce Gibson. *The Cowgirls*. Houston: Cordovan Corporation, 1977.

Sandoz, Mari. The Cattlemen. Lincoln: University of Nebraska Press, Bison edition, 1950.

Sedacek, Signe N., Chairwoman. *Grit, Guts & Gusto: A History of Hill County*. Havre: The Hill County Bicentennial Commission, 1976.

Smith, Helena Huntington. *The War on Powder River*. Norman: University of Nebraska Press, Bison Book, 1966.

Stiffler, Liz, and Tona Blake. "Fannie Sperry-Steele: Montana's Champion Bronc Rider," *Montana: The Magazine of Western History*, Spring 1982.

Urbanek, Mac. *Wyoming Place Names*. Missoula: Mountain Press, 1998.

Wallace, Charles. *The Cattle Queen of Montana: A Story of the Personal Experiences of Mrs. Nate Collins [Elizabeth Smith]*. St. James, MN: Charles Foote, Publisher, 1894.

Werner, Herman. *On the Western Frontier with the United States Infantry—Fifty Years Ago*. Privately published, 1934.

Wilson, Gary A. *Honky-Tonk Town: Havre, Montana's Lawless Era*. Guilford, CT: Helena, MT: Two Dot Imprint, Globe-Pequot Press, 2006.

Wilson, Gary A. "Lee 'The Trader' Grant Runs Local Post," *Bear Paw Sentinel* (Havre, MT) July 15, 1981.

Newspapers
   Billings (MT) Gazette
   Buffalo (WY) News
   Buffalo (WY) Voice
   Casper (WY) Daily Tribune
   Cheyenne (WY) Daily State Leader
   Chinook (MT) Opinion

Cody (WY) Enterprise
Douglas Converse County (WY) Budget
Fort Benton (MT) Record
River Press (Fort Benton, MT)
Gillette (WY) Record News
Glasgow (MT) Courier
Great Falls (MT) Tribune
Havre (MT) Daily News
Havre (MT) Plaindealer
Hi-Line Herald (Havre, MT)
Kansas City (MO) Star
Kaycee (WY) Optimist
Little Rockies (MT) Miner
Malta (MT) Enterprise
Mercury News (San Jose, CA)
Miles City (MT) Daily Star
Milk River Eagle (Havre, MT)
News Record (Renton, WA)
Post Oregonian (Portland, OR)
Promoter-News (Havre, MT)
Record Chronicle (Renton, WA)
Roosevelt County (MT) Independent
Roundup (MT) Tribune
Sheridan (WY) Post-Enterprise
Wyoming Eagle (Laramie, WY)
Wolf Point (MT) Herald

Individuals and Institutions
Anderson, J. & R. families, Toledo (Hill County), MT.
Brady, Francine, author interview.
Briese, Darrel, Havre, MT.
Chandler, Sean, Indian Studies Director/Faculty, Aaniih Nakoda College (formerly Fort Belknap College), Harlem, MT.
Chvilicek, Loy. Pioneer Montana women's researcher, Helena and Havre.
Cypress Hills Provincial Park, The Métis people of the Cypress Hills, Elkwater, Alberta and Maple Creek, Saskatchewan.
Darling, Marvin, Columbia Falls, MT.
Darling, Pat, Bigfork, MT.
Diocese of Great Falls–Billings Archives.
English, Eva, Librarian, Fort Belknap College, Harlem, MT.

First United Methodist Church & Archives, Havre, MT.

Fischer, Dorothy, Billings, MT. Author interview.

Genger, Nancy Grant, Deer Lodge, MT. Author interview.

Gonzaga University, Special Collections Department, Foley Center, Spokane, WA.

Grant, Gary, Havre, MT. Author interview.

Grant, Lee, Havre, MT. Author interview.

Havre High School, Jim Magera's History Class, oral history tapes: Gary Grant interview by L.E. Kanning, May 1997; Lee Grant interview by Lisa Bendo, April 1995; Lee Grant interview by Andy Smith, May 1990.

Havre-Hill County Library: Bonnie Williamson, Francine Brady and staff.

Helland, Mary, Pioneer Museum, Glasgow, MT.

Jellem, Karen, Milk River Genealogical Society, Chinook, MT.

Johnson County (WY) Library: Nancy Jennings.

Kanning, Lori Grant, Havre, MT. Author interview.

Lambert (Montana) Museum & Historical Society.

Lambert, Patricia.

Magera, Jim, Havre, MT.

Mavity, Lyn, Sidney, MT.

Moran, Sharon Logan, Chinook, MT

Patrick, Kathy, Pioneer Montana women's researcher, Helena.

Presser, Marvin, Wolf Point, MT.

Ranger, Jeff, Helena, MT. Author interview.

Roundup–Musselshell Historical Society and Public Library: Dale Algor, Bonnie De Malo, and Shirley Parrot

St. Jude Catholic Church, Havre, MT.

Sheppard, Jude, Blaine County Museum, Chinook.

Spangelo, Jim, Havre, MT.

Taylor, Colin, Casper, WY.

Thompson-Lacey, Caroline, Kennewick, WA, July 27, 1977. Letter to Elaine Thompson, Chinook, MT, containing genealogy information.

Thompson, Elaine, Chinook, MT.

Torgerson, Kenneth.

Trotter, Diane, University of Wyoming Library at Laramie.

Vandeberg, Debbie Grant, Havre, MT. Author interview.

Index

About the Author

Gary A. Wilson is a biographer, historian, and publisher, who has been researching the history of northern Montana and the American West since 1978. He is a founding board member of the Fort Assinniboine Preservation Association, and he is active in several local tourist and historical organizations. Wilson lives in Havre, Montana.

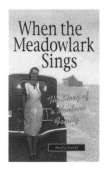
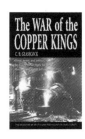
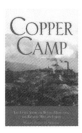